PR
4231
C 57   Cohen, J.M.

Robert Browning

DATE DUE			
MAY 27 70			
MAY 28 71			
APR 28 76			
MAR 18 1980			
MAY 20 1981			
APR 18 86			
NOV 11 1991			
NOV 2 1994			
AUG 13 1997			
APR 14 1999			

WITHDRAWN
Waubonsee Community College

ROBERT BROWNING

ROBERT BROWNING

by
J. M. COHEN

LONGMANS

LONGMANS, GREEN AND CO LTD
48 Grosvenor Street, London W.1
*Associated companies, branches and representatives
throughout the world*

*First published in 1952
Second impression 1964*

PRINTED IN GREAT BRITAIN
BY JOHN DICKENS & CO LTD, NORTHAMPTON

To

EDWARD UPWARD

in friendship

FOREWORD

In striking the balance between 'Man' and 'Book' I have in this study come down deliberately on the side of 'Book', in the first place because the story of Robert Browning's life has been very often told already, and secondly because I have found in his poetry much that seems to me to throw entirely new light on the man. Indeed, by looking once more into the detail of his chief poems from a contemporary standpoint, I believe that I have made some contribution towards a re-estimate of this most seriously underrated of the great Victorians—and that is more than sufficient justification for this book.

My second chapter is based on material from an article on 'The Young Robert Browning,' contributed to *The Cornhill* (No. 975 Summer 1948). I owe my thanks to the proprietors of that journal for permission to make fresh use of it. I have not, however, incorporated it in the form in which it was printed. For in continuing to re-read Browning's poetry, I have had cause to modify some of my previous findings. In that article, as I look back on it, I seem to have been too much concerned with Browning's failure as a Romantic to give proper weight to his tremendous achievement in the field beyond Romanticism. Now, in a complete study, I hope that I have set right my original misjudgment.

J. M. C.

CONTENTS

	FOREWORD	*page* vi
I.	A CLAIM FOR ROBERT BROWNING	1
II.	THE HALF-HEARTED REBEL	11
III.	ALLIANCE OF POETS	46
IV.	SONG'S OUR ART	73
V.	THE ROUGH ORE ROUNDED	104
VI.	SUBJECTS CLASSICAL AND SENSATIONAL	131
VII.	LAST PARLEYINGS OF A SOLITARY MAN	161
VIII.	THE UNACKNOWLEDGED MASTER	174
	SHORT BIBLIOGRAPHY	194
	INDEX	197

Chapter One

A CLAIM FOR ROBERT BROWNING

No major English poet is worse served by the anthologist than is Robert Browning. He has few perfect lyrics to offer, for primarily he is not a lyric poet at all. His work is always on a bold scale which faces the anthologist with the alternatives of drastically cutting, of omitting, or of including poems that are short but not of his best. Hence the constant inclusion of 'Home Thoughts from the Sea,' of 'The Lost Leader,' and even of that juvenile and unrepresentative horror-poem, 'Porphyria's Lover.' But most damaging of all to Browning's reputation is the too frequent appearance of 'Pippa's Song':

> God's in his heaven—
> All's right with the world!

The contemporary reader finds it hard to forgive Robert Browning the optimism of those two lines. But Pippa speaks for one side of Browning's nature only, voices only his simple belief in a certain primal innocence, of which he made her the symbol. He was, nevertheless, at heart an optimist, though of a far from naïve kind. He certainly believed that there is no virtue in doubt, and that behind the apparent disorder and contradictions of earthly events there is both a meaning and a purpose. But smug or facile he certainly was not. Would his greatest poem be concerned with the callous murder of an innocent woman if the whole of his experience could be summed up in the comforting affirmation that all is right with the world? There is a great deal of evil in the world of *The Ring and the Book*, but three lives are redeemed from their various depths of squalor and sin by the example of Pompilia's suffering and death. The snap judgment which has gone against Browning will not survive a reading of even one chapter of his masterpiece. Besides, do we require all our poets to recommend an early suicide?

Browning has suffered worse even than Spenser at the hands of the anthologist. He has suffered too from the strait-jacket of the printer's double column. Anyone wishing to read him in comfort would do well to use the seventeen volume collected edition, which is still to be picked up cheaply in second-hand bookshops, or to purchase the recent *Reynard* selection, a note of which he will find in my concluding bibliography.

But Browning has one advantage over such comparatively unanthologized poets as Spenser and the mature Milton of *Paradise Lost*: that we have met him in youth. Now both the familiar 'Pied Piper,' and the hardly less familiar 'How they brought the good News from Ghent to Aix,' are poems of tremendous accomplishment. They are, in fact, almost the only poems of their age that tell a story with something of a ballad monger's directness. Rossetti, William Morris and Swinburne tried to revive the ballad form and failed, because the medium was now artificial, and their treatment of it archaic. If a new Robin Hood or Sir Patrick Spens were to be added to the figures of popular imagination, the poet would require a different language, and one closer to the rhythms of the music hall song, or to saloon bar conversation, with which to work the miracle. In fact the

A Claim for Robert Browning

miracle never took place; society was too widely split by differences in interest and education for the poet to appeal to any but a middle-class audience. But Thomas Hood's apprenticeship to the music hall, his writing of sketches and songs to be presented by the popular comedian Charles Matthews, vastly extended the vocabulary, the metres and the allusiveness of nineteenth-century poetry. This new capital, of which Hood himself lived to make very little use, was taken over by Browning for such a poem as the 'Pied Piper,' and finally developed into a medium capable of expressing far greater psychological accuracy, of referring to far more things in a far less 'poetical' way than any other Victorian poet could achieve. Anyone comparing the nimble argument of *The Ring and the Book* with the conventional narrative flow of *The Idylls of the King* will realize the point of this argument, which I shall develop at length in later chapters. Browning took over from Hood—and incidentally passed on to Ezra Pound and so to our day—rhythms halfway between the spoken and the dramatic—between Charles Matthews' and Shakespeare's, in much the same way as Jules Laforgue, a later and more widely acknowledged ancestor of modern poetry, took elements from the French music halls, nursery rhyme and popular song which have passed from him to T. S. Eliot and so to W. H. Auden, and which still persist in contemporary French poetry.

'The Pied Piper' is an important poem and a very entertaining one, but it is not a great one. Browning did not write great poetry until he had attained emotional maturity, and this he lacked till the years of his marriage. Browning till thirty-five was a minor Romantic, whose single deep experience was his failure to make the Romantic rebellion against religion, society and parental standards, made with varying degrees of violence by Wordsworth, Shelley and Byron. Browning came of middle-class nonconformist stock, and inherited a liberal background far more difficult to revolt against than the squirearchical Toryism from which other Romantics had sprung. Browning, besides, was lucky in his parents, and fortunate in being allowed to choose for himself the type of education that suited him. He was, however, slow in attaining the depths of experience which poetry requires. Had he died at the age of Shelley or Keats or even Byron, he would appear today a very minor figure in the Victorian field, the author of an obscure narrative poem lit with flashes of brilliant description—*Sordello*; of a promising but uneven verse drama—*Pippa Passes*; and of a dozen or two fine lyrics that are none of them word perfect, all of them a little rough in finish. For, as has been said, Browning was not an accomplished poet on a small scale. He was an adventurous poet, at his best only when handling large conceptions.

His true poetry, when it came, was the poetry of maturity, which is, perhaps, one of the reasons why the present age is reluctant to recognize its worth. For ours is an intellectually over-ripe but emotionally underdeveloped civilization. Browning's poetry is mature in that he does not self-dramatize; *Pauline*—his earliest poem and one which despite its beauties he would have discarded if he could—is the only considerable work in which 'Robert Browning, poet' monopolizes the foreground. He was not, on the other hand, content to be a mere objective story-teller, as he had been in 'The Pied Piper,' which, incidentally, he had composed only to amuse a sick child. Browning invented characters whom he could use as his mouthpieces to express various attitudes to life. These attitudes were all, no doubt, his own at certain times and under certain circumstances. But he was not interested in them merely on that account. Indeed, as this book will show, he was reluctant to acknowledge that his 'Men and Women' were speaking for himself. Yet of all his critics his French friend Joseph Milsand was the only one whose judgments he wholeheartedly accepted, and Milsand clearly saw the connection between his characters and the various personalities of which he was composed. Indeed Browning tacitly acknowledged the truth of Milsand's argument by the form and nature of his greatest poem, *The Ring and the Book*, in which he succeeded in grouping a number of personages around a central event—as he might a number of his own component personalities around a more permanent self—and thereby presented not only a wide canvas, a canvas as rich and various as that of Frith's *Derby Day*, but one at the same time which conveyed an unity greater than that of a mere group of people all standing at the same place and facing in the same direction. The personages involved in the case of Guido Franceschini are not merely found together on the same day in a Roman court of law. They are not merely witnesses to the same set of facts. Their unity lies in their having, each of them, witnessed a miracle; and the miracle is Pompilia. Never did the great Victorian writers fail so disastrously as when they attempted to present 'a pure woman.' Usually the cause of the trouble was their identification of purity with sexual immaturity. But Pompilia's purity was of a different kind. It lay in her selflessness, first displayed towards her brutal husband and then in the interests of her child. Her transforming effect upon the worldly priest, upon the ageing and still doubting Pope, and finally on her husband and murderer himself, derived from the quality of her own emotion. She represented a depth of experience greater than theirs that they could not fail to be conscious of, and Browning was able to convey that difference in quality.

It was not that he was a man with first-hand religious experience. He remained a doubter to the end, and if ever he ventured to affirm more than he knew the resulting falsity in his poetry is easy to detect. But Browning, at his best, could express the whole of his experience of love, faith and creative power, which were the three poles upon which his universe hung. He was capable of faithfully recording such flashes of emotion as he had. The nature of his experience, and its relationship to his poetry, it is the business of later chapters to set out.

Browning was a poet of considerable intellectual ingenuity, but he was not a philospher; he makes no general statements about man's place in the world. His reasoning is at its subtlest when he is presenting a case, the case for the cautious yet combative Bishop Blougram, content to believe less than he claimed to, yet firmly convinced of the necessity of belief, or the case of Karshish the Physician, anxious to adhere to a purely scientific standpoint even when confronted with the miracle of Lazarus, which fell outside the province of the scientifically explicable. Both are invented characters in the same sense as is 'The Pied Piper'; yet both stand for elements in Browning's own thought, and in the thought of his age, that could be more succinctly and more completely presented in the form of a poem than in that of a prose argument, worldly-Catholic, positivist or otherwise. Blougram, Karshish, Cleon, Andrea del Sarto, are independent characters, facets of the poet himself and at the same time representative

A Claim for Robert Browning

figures of his own time. All of them are to a lesser or greater degree taken up with one of the principal problems of nineteenth-century thought: the question whether art rather than religion is not the highest experience of which man is aware. To this heresy Browning did not subscribe.

But Browning's poems have greater claims on the reader than their mere concern with the problems of their day, and their success in stating these problems without suggesting any premature or facile solution. They are the poems of a mature poet, in whom thought, emotion and sensation are in a state of equipoise. Browning was not predominantly an intellectual poet as was Clough; nor did his work express only his rare intimations of some divine order behind the apparent confusion of earthly life as did Christina Rossetti's; nor did he draw only upon the richness and beauty of the world without, and of its impression upon his senses, as did Alfred Tennyson at his best. In Browning's poetry the three faculties of thought, feeling and sense are brought into play, as can perhaps best be demonstrated by taking some almost random quotations from the body of his work.

First let me choose a piece of close-knit reasoning, in which the Pope in *The Ring and the Book* speculates upon the small effect that Christianity has had upon the world:

> And is this little all that was to be?
> Where is the gloriously-decisive change,
> Metamorphosis the immeasurable
> Of human clay to divine gold, we looked
> Should, in some poor sort, justify its price?
> Had an adept of the mere Rosy Cross[1]

[1] A member of the Rosicrucian Society, practitioners in alchemy (The Great Work).

Spent his life to consummate the Great Work,
Would not we start to see the stuff it touched
Yield not a grain more than the vulgar got
By the old smelting-process years ago?
If this were sad to see in just the sage
Who should profess so much, perform no more,
What is it when suspected in that Power
Who undertook to make and made the world,
Devised and did effect man, body and soul,
Ordained salvation for them both, and yet . . .
Well, is the thing we see, salvation?

I

Put no such dreadful question to myself,
Within whose circle of experience burns
I must outlive a thing ere know it dead . . .
The central truth, Power, Wisdom, Goodness,—God:

Again, for depth of feeling there is a little known lyric of the poet's old age, from *Ferishtah's Fancies*, which shall serve:

Not with my Soul, Love!—bid no Soul like mine
   Lap thee around nor leave the poor sense room!
Soul,—travel-worn, toil-weary,—would confine
   Along with Soul, Soul's gains from glow and gloom,
Captures from soarings high and divings deep.
Spoil-laden Soul, how should such memories sleep?
Take Sense, too—let me love entire and whole—
   Not with my Soul!

Eyes shall meet eyes and find no eyes between,
   Lips feed on lips, no other lips to fear!
No past, no future—so thine arms but screen
   The present from surprise! not there, 'tis here—
Not then, 'tis now:—back, memories that intrude!
Make, Love, the universe our solitude,
And, over all the rest, oblivion roll—
   Sense quenching Soul!

A Claim for Robert Browning

As for Browning's rejoicing in the manifold richness of the visible world, this was present in his poetry from the beginning to the end, from *Pauline*, out of which I draw my next quotation, to the 'Parleying with Gerard de Lairesse' which yields me my last.

> See this our new retreat
> Walled in with a sloped mound of matted shrubs,
> Dark, tangled, old and green, still sloping down
> To a small pool whose waters lie asleep
> Amid the trailing boughs turned water-plants:
> And tall trees overarch to keep us in,
> Breaking the sunbeams into emerald shafts,
> And in the dreamy water one small group
> Of two or three strange trees are got together
> Wondering at all around, as strange beasts herd
> Together far from their own land: all wildness,
> No turf nor moss, for boughs and plants pave all,
> And tongues of bank go shelving in the lymph,
> Where the pale-throated snake reclines his head,
> And old grey stones lie making eddies there,
> The wild-mice cross them dry-shod.

Noon is the conqueror,—not a spray, nor leaf,
Nor herb, nor blossom but has rendered up
Its morning dew: the valley seemed one cup
Of cloud-smoke, but the vapour's reign was brief,
Sun-smitten, see, it hangs—the filmy haze—
Grey-garmenting the herbless mountain-side,
To soothe the day's sharp glare: while far and wide
Above unclouded burns the sky, one blaze
With fierce immitigable blue, no bird
Ventures to spot by passage. E'en of peaks
Which still presume there, plain each pale point
    speaks
In wan transparency of waste incurred

> By over-daring: far from me be such!
> Deep in the hollow, rather, where combine
> Tree, shrub and briar to roof with shade and cool
> The remnant of some lily-strangled pool,
> Edged round with mossy fringing soft and fine.
> Smooth lie the bottom slabs, and overhead
> Watch elder, bramble, rose, and service-tree
> And one beneficent rich barberry
> Jewelled all over with fruit-pendents red.

A poet capable of these four passages, carelessly chosen out of his super-abundance, deserves, surely more than any other of the great Victorians, a re-reading and re-assessment. Perhaps the following chapters will do a little towards restoring his reputation, and towards showing the relevance of his poetry to our contemporary scene. For my purpose is to guide readers back to one of the greatest of English poets.

Chapter Two

THE HALF-HEARTED REBEL

IN the spring of 1887, just before his seventy-fifth birthday, Robert Browning published his last book but one, *Parleyings with Certain People of Importance in their Day*. In their day, however, the importance of his people had not been great; it was for their significance to him in his own far-away boyhood that he clothed these scarcely surviving shadows each with a robust and disputatious personality. Bernard de Mandeville, Daniel Bartoli, Christopher Smart, George Bubb Doddington, what were they now but names on the spine of some almost forgotten book or, in Doddington's case, attached to a story of political failure? It was in order to evoke the thoughts and emotions of his own early years that Browning summoned them for parley. The *Parleyings* were his *Dichtung und Wahrheit*, an attempt by calling up pictures from the past to gain a clearer view of his long life's course. This need imaginatively to relive experiences now much more than half a century old was one characteristic—and by no means an isolated one—common to Goethe and Browning; it is perhaps a need common to man, to see his life as a whole before leaving it, and to endeavour to understand, if only dimly, the pattern and purpose of his days. Goethe and Browning, however, adopted widely divergent methods of exploration. *Dichtung und Wahrheit* is an autobiographical reconstruction; facts are arranged in the light of a poetic insight into significance. Browning, on the other hand, had no wish to recall sixty-year old events. Everything had led up to the supreme experience of his love for Elizabeth Barrett, and to its counterparts in poetry, *Men and Women* and *The Ring and the Book*. Moreover, from the outset, he had been chary of self-revelations.

> Outside should suffice for evidence:
> And whoso desires to penetrate
> Deeper, must dive by the spirit-sense—
> No optics like yours, at any rate!

So, in the poem 'House,' he warned off the curious for personal ancedote and public introspection. What he sought to recapture in the *Parleyings* was rather former states of mind than the details of far away happenings.

Browning's 'People of Importance' were therefore, in the words of his friend and biographer Mrs. Sutherland Orr, 'men whose works connected themselves with the intellectual sympathies and the imaginative pleasures of his very earliest youth.' 'He had summoned them up,' she wrote, 'not for the sake of drawing their portraits, but that they might help him to draw his own;' and for that purpose none could be fitter than the authors in his father's library at their home in Southampton Street, Camberwell, and the painters in the Dulwich Public Gallery. For Robert Browning's education owed little to school or college. 'Italy was my university,' he would say in later years, when asked whether he had been to Oxford or Cambridge. His tastes and interests were formed, however, long before he visited Italy. They took shape in the years of his precocious reading recalled in the *Parleyings*.

Browning's first three poems, *Pauline*, *Paracelsus*, and *Sordello*, though none of them successful as a whole,

The Half-hearted Rebel

nevertheless all contain passages that only a poet of deep, though inchoate, feeling could have written. *Pauline*, in fact, comes near—in parts—to achieving mastery in the field of romantic self-dramatization, which Browning very deliberately eschewed in everything that he wrote thereafter. Its tone is pessimistic. The young poet— he was twenty when he wrote it—monopolizes the poem's foreground, dwarfing his dimly outlined mistress Pauline, till she is no more than a stage property. Its setting is autumn, the verse a weak variant of the measure of 'Alastor,' and the driving force a sense of sin projected upon the imaginary poet, its hero, but clearly at that time dominant in Browning's own mind. This first poem betrays no foreshadowing of the sense of character, the dramatic speech, or the wealth of detail that characterize the later Browning. It is the poetry of mood. But like all Browning's work it is remarkable for a unity of texture, which is unbroken, though the verse falls and rises in its emotional intensity from derivative flatness and self-pity to aggressive self-assertion: contrasting strains which are reconciled only upon a note of generalized hope, so inconclusive that it is impossible to be certain from the poem whether the young poet is intended to have died or survived. '*Pauline* is *the* one of Mr. Browning's longer poems of which no intelligible abstract is possible,' wrote Mrs. Sutherland Orr. One figure, however, does emerge from this shapeless confession, that of Shelley, whose example is invoked in a passage which sheds some light on the mind of the young Browning:

> Sun-treader, I believe in God and truth
> And love; and as one just escaped from death
> Would bind himself in bands of friends to feel
> He lives indeed, so, I would lean on thee!

It is in his attitude to the dead poet that Browning gives us the clue to his own malaise. The sin of which he accused himself, in the person of the poet in *Pauline*, was pride or self-will, and the embodiment of these was Shelley.

The young Browning was at one with his dissenting parents in accepting the Christian ethic, if not the letter of the creed, Nor had he carried through the normal adolescent revolt against their standards and authority. He had, none the less, at the age of fourteen, seized upon 'Mr. Shelley's atheistical poem,' *Queen Mab*, in a box of second-hand books, and for perhaps as much as two years remained 'a professing atheist and a practising vegetarian,' writes Mrs. Orr. Yet this seems to have drawn down no parental disapproval. His mother procured for him the rest of Shelley's works and, on the book-seller's recommendation, some volumes of Keats as well. His careful education at home was not interrupted by this juvenile passion. Mr. Browning approved his son's ambition to make poetry a career. He himself held a clerkship in the Bank of England, then a lucrative post, but he considered that such work might prove too monotonous for his son; and though both the law and diplomacy seemed at times possible careers for young Robert, no one seems to have questioned the suitability of the son's living on at his father's expense, first at Camberwell and later at Hatcham, until at the age of thirty-four he made his runaway marriage with Elizabeth Barrett. Throughout his life his sister Sarianne, who was some years his junior, remained his closest friend.

Browning soon forsook his Shelleyan atheism, and adapted himself to the parental standards, yet there is evidence in *Pauline* that the adjustment was not made without spiritual cost.

The Half-hearted Rebel

The central figure of Browning's next poem, *Paracelsus*, written two years later, partakes both of Faust and Prometheus; it is a study in the Romantic sin of intellectual pride—a theme less closely related to the poet's own experience than the Shelleyan enthusiasm of *Pauline*. Though boldly planned, *Paracelsus* is deficient in dramatic development, and its hero's ultimate defeat is so long expected than when it comes it lacks all elements of tragedy. Less mawkish than *Pauline*, this second poem has also less emotional tension; its conception is too patently an intellectual one. Though, unlike its predecessor, it could be reduced to an intelligible abstract, its plot would seem, when baldly stated, to be repeatedly turning back on itself. Nor has this poem any passages as fine as the best of *Pauline*. Browning had abandoned his Romantic style without achieving any compensating individuality. Even the best of *Paracelsus* is, indeed, rather further from the mature Browning idiom than such a descriptive passage from *Pauline* as that quoted at the end of the last chapter. It is reminiscent rather, as Edmund Gosse observed, of the monstrous family of *Festuses*, *Balders* and *Life Dramas*—pretentious works of that day which owed their popularity to a false show of profundity and to an utter flatness of style which made them comprehensible to a newly literate audience incapable of understanding poetry of any complexity. Browning, however, was still not sufficiently plain to rival the masters of that 'Spasmodic' school—Alexander Smith, R. H. Horne and P. J. Bailey. *Paracelsus* found him no readers. The explanation lies in an aloofness in the poet that had not grown less in the two years since the writing of *Pauline*. He had by now made friends with a number of young men with intellectual interests, chief among whom were Alfred Domett—the Waring of a later poem—and Joseph Arnould. Yet he seems to have remained emotionally isolated and to have found social intercourse difficult, since even as late as 1840 he wrote to Domett on the subject of *Sordello*, 'the fact is I live by myself, write with no better company, and forget that the *lovers* you mention'—the characters in the poem —'are part and parcel of that self, and their choosing to comprehend my comprehensions but an indifferent testimony to their value . . .'

This aloofness is the true subject of the poem. It is in fact the principle constituent of that pride which led to Paracelsus's fall. 'A being knowing not what love is,' he is consumed by a passion for intellectual knowledge, and by a longing to perform some signal deed which will earn him mankind's admiration. But it is his own isolated ambition that the poet is voicing in an exaggerated form when he makes his hero cry:

>   I seemed to long
> At once to trample on, yet save mankind,
> To make some unexampled sacrifice
> In their behalf, to wring some wondrous good
> From heaven or earth for them, to perish, winning
> Eternal weal in the act . . .
> Yet never to be mixed with men so much
> As to have part even in my own work, share
> In my own largess . . .

Against this attitude of contemptuous benevolence Festus, Michal and Aprile—the other shadowy characters in the poem—all stand for the power of love. To the young Browning creation and love of his fellow men stood on one side, the scientific pursuit of knowledge on the other; and neither alone was sufficient. It is only after his acknowledgment of this truth that Paracelsus can finally claim, as he lies dying, to have attained some

The Half-hearted Rebel

vision or certainty, unclear to the poet himself and consequently unconvincing to the reader. Yet though the nature of Paracelsus's attainment remains mysterious to the end his final speech does more than merely bring a long and shapeless poem to some sort of conclusion. It adumbrates the course that Browning was himself to pursue in his maturity.

> Let men
> Regard me, and the poet dead long ago
> Who loved too rashly; and shape forth a third
> And better-tempered spirit, warned by both
> As from the over-radiant star too mad
> To drink the life-springs, beamless thence itself—
> And the dark orb which borders the abyss,
> Ingulfed in icy night—might have its course
> A temperate and equidistant world.

'A temperate and equidistant world': so would the intricate landscape of *Men and Women* have appeared, viewed from the cloudy heights on which the young poet dwelt with his Promethean hero. Moreover, as the last quotation suggests, the young Browning half foresaw where his future kingdom lay.

The critics wrote *Paracelsus* down as Shelleyan. Elizabeth Barrett, however, could not accept the verdict of its derivativeness. 'An imitation of Shelley!' she protested in the course of their correspondence, 'when if *Paracelsus* was anything it was the expression of a new mind, as all might see, as *I* saw, let me be proud to remember.' But *Paracelsus*, though certainly the expression of a new mind, was too large and too theoretical in conception. Browning's originality was still unequal to a poem on this scale. Nor was his technique sufficiently developed. The blank verse does not yet bear his characteristic rough-cast texture; it is too smooth to match the ruggedness of his thought, which thereby suffers a loosely rhetorical weakening.

Browning's interest in the theatre had begun in his boyhood. The poem *Pauline* is dated 'Richmond, 22 October, 1832,' on which night he had gone with some cousins to the little theatre on Richmond Green, where Edmund Kean, some six months before his death, was playing Richard III. That night, Browning noted in his own copy of his first poem, he conceived the idea of writing it and others. 'I don't know whether I had not made up my mind to *act* as well as to make verses, music and God knows what,—*que de châteaux en Espagne!*'

Meanwhile the poet was making a wider circle of acquaintances; through an old friend he met the actor-manager William Macready, and through him John Forster, the future biographer of Dickens. Forster was writing a life of Strafford, which Browning revised for him during the author's illness, and Macready, as manager of Covent Garden, was championing the true drama against the spectacles and melodramas put on by the other licensed theatre, Drury Lane.

Browning was at that time, in the words of a young woman friend, 'slim and dark and very handsome and, may I hint it? just a trifle of a dandy, addicted to lemon-coloured kid gloves and such things: quite the glass of fashion and the mould of form. But full of ambition, eager for success, eager for fame and, what is more, determined to conquer fame and to achieve success.' To this young man Macready turned to save, if not the English theatre, at least his tenure of Covent Garden. 'He looks and speaks more like a poet than any man I ever saw,' he wrote. But a dramatic presence, though sufficient perhaps to account for the actor-manager's spontaneous invitation to write him a play, was no evidence that the young man had a dramatist's gifts. *Strafford*, the play he wrote, proved that he had not. Its situations are wooden and its lines undistinguished; it is mere prose chopped to blank verse length. Though not damned on its first presentation, with Macready in the title role, it did not last beyond five performances. Browning swore that he would never write another. But his friendship with Macready and the fascination of the theatre prevented his keeping to his resolution.

For the moment he returned to his poem *Sordello*, which he published in 1840. The Paracelsus in him was far from written out and the new poem is, like its predecessors, a confession of defeat, this time of failure to translate dream into action. In the course of the whole tale the poet Sordello emerges only twice from his subjective world. The stress of the poem, Browning declared in a later preface to it, was 'on the incidents in the development of a soul, little else being worth the study;' which last is as well, for the detail of the story is most obscure, partly owing to a too great allusiveness, and partly because of the abrupt transitions in the narrative. But in one way *Sordello* is an advance on the more diffuse and straightforward *Paracelsus*. Eglamor, the poetic craftsman talented but uninspired, Naddo, the critic, and Salinguerra, the Renaissance chieftain who proves to be Sordello's father, are round characters foreshadowing the great figures in *Men and Women*. The Italian background too is revealed in flashes of lovely detail, more clearly defined than the generalized landscape which occasionally leaps into being behind the larger-than-life figure of *Paracelsus*. *Sordello* was largely written before the poet's first visit to Italy, the impressions of which are more deeply stamped on *Pippa Passes*; but it is no exaggeration to say that the imaginary thirteenth-century background of the first poem is as real as the observed nineteenth-century detail of the second. How deeply significant the creation of Sordello's world was for Browning may be deduced from the fact that it is here that his first profoundly individual writing appears, in lines where the exact eye of a Crabbe, the emotional force of Shelley, and a compact reasoning akin to Shakespeare's combine to form something new in English poetry. It is hard to substantiate this claim by the choice of a short passage, and it is only in flashes that poetry emerges from the poem's packed and turgid detail; but if a few lines must serve for example, let it be a description early in the second book:

>   wide
> Opened the great morass, shot every side
> With flashing water through and through; a-shine,
> Thick-steaming, all-alive. Whose shape divine,
> Quivered i' the farthest rainbow-vapour, glanced
> Athwart the flying herons? He advanced,
> But warily; though Mincio leaped no more,
> Each foot-fall burst up in the marish-floor
> A diamond jet . . .

Here are the beginnings of an original style, and elsewhere in *Sordello* are the first adumbrations of Browning's characteristic irony.

But the poem is inextricably difficult, a clear proof of the poet's statement to Domett already quoted, that he lived by himself. In this state of mind he had made a solitary three months' journey to Italy, setting out in April 1838, after the failure of *Strafford*, carrying in his head this poem whose primary narrative interest to him had long ago been overlaid by the accretions of secondary incidents and of introspections concerning the best method of presentation. Yet *Sordello* is, with all its

The Half-hearted Rebel

obscurities, a far better poem than either *Pauline* or *Paracelsus*. Browning wove his texture too tight, but a tautening was necessary. Its failure lies in his incapacity, at that time, to draw with a firm outline.

Perhaps, too, in his pride, and in his disappointment at his failure to find a ready public, he was inclined to be uncompromising, or even to try and shock his reader; perhaps something in him urged him not to make himself plain, to hide his meaning. Writing of society in general to Elizabeth Barrett some years later, he observed: 'For me, I always hated it—have put up with it these six or seven years past, lest by foregoing it I should let some unknown God escape me.' It was perhaps his search for an unknown goddess, foreshadowed in *Pauline*, rather than any love of his fellow men that drew Robert Browning into society.

By the time he wrote that letter he was anxious to make *Sordello* more readable. It had met with blank incomprehension from most who had seen it; even Tennyson, who admired him, made the well-known and often repeated quip that he only understood two lines of it—the opening 'Who will may hear Sordello's story told,' and the final, 'Who would has heard Sordello's story told'—and that these were both lies. Carlyle reported that his wife had read it through without being able to make out whether Sordello was a man or a city or a book. Browning later proposed to Elizabeth that he should clarify the poem by expanding it. She, however, wanted him to draw it together and fortify the connections and associations, but in the end nothing was done. In his 1863 dedication he excused his faults of expression, and claimed that he had written it only for a few.

On his return from Italy, Browning, to the neglect of his poetry, started work on two historical pieces, *King*

Victor and King Charles and *The Return of the Druses*. *King Victor and King Charles* was a romantic chronicle play whose plot adhered closely to the anecdote on which it was based. But *The Return of the Druses* was a more ambitious play with an oriental setting, on a subject, in Browning's own words, 'of the most wild and passionate love' rising to extremes of 'self devotement and self-forgetting.' Macready seems to have been against the piece from the start, though had its author possessed a little dramatic ability the plot might have been worked up into quite a colourful melodrama. Certainly Browning did not fail through making concessions to his own taste; he was bent on a stage triumph, and the verse he wrote was plain enough even for the most inexperienced actors. The play's lack of construction, however, was its undoing. Its action is repeatedly held up by soliloquies and asides. Dramatic development is almost entirely lacking. So static is *The Return of the Druses*, indeed, that it is possible to read act five immediately after act one without missing anything of importance. Macready rejected it, as well as the less ambitious *King Victor and King Charles*, as more suitable for the study than the stage. Unfortunately, however, in his endeavour to write plays crude enough for the stage, Browning had produced something too thin and declamatory for any reader.

Fortunately, Robert Browning did not confine himself to attempts at winning stage success. During long walks about the countryside, often taken at night, which he enjoyed as a contrast to his theatrical preoccupations in London, he began to compose a number of lyrics and a long poem conceived in dramatic form though lyrical in texture, which were to excel anything he had so far written. This poem *Pippa Passes*, of 1841, was rich with

The Half-hearted Rebel

the inspiration he had found in Italy. But, more important still, it introduced a new theme into his writing, the motif of innocence, which contrasts most strongly with the general feeling of self-reproach and the sense of failure that colour *Pauline*, *Paracelsus* and *Sordello*. *Pippa Passes* marks the first stage of Browning's emergence from his Romanticism. In conceiving an image of purity with which to confront the nightmare world of the strange and morbid that he had brought to light in his two 'Madhouse Cells' lyrics—'Johannes Agricola' and 'Porphyria's Lover'—and that recurs even in *Pippa* in the scene between Ottima and Sebald, he had drawn for the first time on the strong and positive side of his own nature.

There could be no greater contrast than that between Porphyria, throttled by her lover with her own hair, or Ottima and Sebald disposing of the body of her murdered husband, on the one side, and Pippa, on the other, the girl from the silk-mills whose holiday it is to live other folks' lives and, by seeing them as more beautiful than they are, by idealizing them for no purpose of her own, to bring benefit to others who do not know of her existence. Pippa is innocence, is poetry. She is the 'third and better-tempered spirit' of Paracelsus's dying speech.

'That little peasant's voice,' breaking in on her one day of holiday, persuades Ottima's lover Sebald to pay the price of his crime, the murder of her husband; prompts the sculptor Jules to accept the bride who has been foisted on him in joke; recalls the patriot Luigi to his duty and awakes the unscrupulous prelate, Monsignor, to the wickedness of the plot which the intendant is proposing to him, to sell Pippa to her death in the brothels of Rome: for unknown to herself, she is the daughter of the priest's elder brother and, as such, heiress to some villas Monsignor expects to revert to him. The plan of the poem is modest and well balanced, and redeemed from sentimentality by Pippa's ironic conviction that the four principal characters are 'Asolo's Four Happiest Ones,' Ottima and Sebald the closest of lovers, Jules and Phene happy on their marriage-day, Luigi and his mother content, and Monsignor—

> —whom they expect from Rome
> To visit Asolo, his brothers' home,
> And say here masses proper to release
> A soul from pain—what storm dares hurt his peace?

As for Pippa herself, on her holiday,

> What shall I please to-day?
> My morn, noon, eve and night—how spend my day?
> Tomorrow I must be Pippa who winds silk,
> The whole year round, to earn just bread and milk:
> But, this one day, I have leave to go
> And play out my fancy's fullest games;
> I may fancy all day—and it shall be so—
> That I taste of the pleasures, am called by the names
> Of the Happiest Four in our Asolo!

This poem was Browning's first completely successful creation, and Pippa the first of his characters to take independent life. For in her he crystallized a personality capable of exorcising that sense of horror and guilt which was his legacy from the half-hearted rebellion of his boyhood. The relationship of the little silk weaver to the guilty lovers foreshadowed, in effect, one aspect of Browning's own attitude to his *Men and Women*, that of the innocent mind which in reflecting evil throws into relief also that vitality and humanity which seem to make

The Half-hearted Rebel

even the most worldly redeemable. Browning had no belief in eternal damnation; Pippa, and later Pompilia, by their purity were capable of saving even such inhuman wretches as Monsignor and Guido Franceschini. But Pippa's creator was not blind to wickedness. In the scene between Ottima and Sebald, which, in Arthur Symons' view, reached the highest level of tragic utterance Browning ever attained, the guilt of their love is expressed in every line, and nowhere more effectively than in their memory of their first secret meetings:

> Buried in woods we lay, you recollect;
> Swift ran the searching tempest overhead;
> And ever and anon some bright white shaft
> Burned thro' the pine-tree roof, here burned and there,
> As if God's messenger thro' the close wood screen
> Plunged and replunged his weapon at a venture,
> Feeling for guilty thee and me: then broke
> The thunder like a whole sea overhead—

Here is the emotional quality of *Pauline* but in more concentrated form, the intensity of 'Porphyria's Lover' without its strained perversity. Browning is now master of an individual line, sometimes rhymed, sometimes unrhymed, less congested than *Sordello*'s. It was with reason that Elizabeth Barrett envied him the writing of this poem, which of all his work she loved best; he himself also valued it above everything else he had produced till then.

Browning's next publication was a collection of sixteen *Dramatic Lyrics*, which contains at least three poems now as well-known as any in the language—'The Soliloquy in the Spanish Cloister,' 'Waring' and 'The Pied Piper of Hamelin.' Yet its most promising feature was the sheer variety of its accomplishment. In his very earliest short poems Browning had cared more for sound than for sense. Now he was master of a free medium in which word-sound certainly guided argument, but in which, far from lulling the ear as in most poetry depending primarily on the music of its words, the metrical devices were used to vary the pace and excitement of the narrative. It is perhaps superfluous to point to the consummate accomplishment of such a passage from 'The Pied Piper' as the one in which the one surviving rat brings home to Rat-land his commentary. But it is important to see what influences Browning was drawing on, to reinvigorate the tired Romanticism which he had inherited. It is too easy to take such familiar lines as these for granted:

> At the first shrill notes of the pipe,
> I heard a sound as of scraping tripe,
> And putting apples, wondrous ripe,
> Into a cider press's gripe:
> And a moving away of pickle-tub-boards,
> And a leaving ajar of conserve-cupboards,
> And a drawing the corks of train-oil-flasks,
> And a breaking the hoops of butter-casks:
> And it seemed as if a voice
> (Sweeter far than by harp or by psaltery
> Is breathed) called out, 'Oh rats, rejoice!
> The world is grown to one vast drysaltery.'

The only contemporary master of such headlong rhythms and of such wealth of rhyme, the only poets then writing with a comparable eye for realistic detail, were Thomas Hood and the Reverend Harris Barham. But they used their medium only for broadly comic purposes; Hood's serious verse is entirely conventional in form. It is most revealing to place beside this impetuous narrative of Browning's, a piece of uncertain mock-romanticism by that master of 'the Comic':

The Half-hearted Rebel

What sort of tricks they mean to play
By way of diversion, who can say,
Of such ferocious and barbarous folk,
Who chuckled, indeed, but never spoke
Of burning Robert the Jäger to coke
Except as a capital practical joke!
Who never thought of Mercy, or heard her,
Or any gentle emotion felt;
But hard as the iron they had to melt,
Sported with Danger and romp'd with Murder!

No one familiar with the *Comic Annuals* will doubt that Hood's example did much to free Browning from conventional forms, and to encourage the tremendous extension of his poetic vocabulary. But the Reverend Harris Barham, the second series of whose *Ingoldsby Legends* appeared in the same year as Browning's *Dramatic Lyrics*, also contributed something to the freedom and daring of 'The Pied Piper's' rhythms, and through them to the rough-cast of the mature Browning's style. The 'Witch's Frolic' runs at the same pace as the rats' helter-skelter rush to their destruction.

On, on to the cellar! away! away!
On, on to the cellar without more delay!
The whole *posse* rush onwards in battle array—
Conceive the dismay of the party so gay,
Old Goody Jones, Goody Price, and Madge Gray,
When the door bursting wide, they descried the allied
Troops, prepared for the onslaught, roll in like a tide,
And the spits, and the tongs, and the pokers beside!—
'Boot and saddle's the word! mount, Cummers, and ride!'—
Alarm was ne'er caused more strong and indigenous
By cats among rats, or a hawk in a pigeon-house;
    Quick from the view
    Away they all flew,
With a yell and a screech and a halliballoo.

'Hey up the chimney! Hey after you!'—
The Volscians themselves made an exit less speedy
From Corioli, 'fluttered like doves' by Macready.

From Hood and from Barham Browning derived that metrical virtuosity which he applied not only to the Hamelin narrative—but also to the poem 'Waring,' addressed to his friend Alfred Domett who had now gone to New Zealand. Here an entire difference of feeling masks the influence of the two master 'Comics.' But it is nevertheless present in such apparently careless lines as these:

> He was prouder then the devil:
> How he must have cursed our revel!
> Ay and many other meetings,
> Indoor visits, outdoor greetings,
> As up and down he paced this London,
> With no work done, but great works undone . . .

Here, however, the influence is almost absorbed, and the mature Browning rough-cast nearly perfected.

Browning's affection for Domett was deeper than any he had so far known. Theirs was a friendship which was to survive long years of separation, and which was resumed when Domett returned to Europe thirty years later. But even more important than the warmth of his affection for his departed friend was Browning's feeling out towards a love to which he aspired, but of which he had so far found no more than a premonitory shadow. Two poems printed under the title 'Queen Worship' show already the transcendental significances with which the young poet endowed the idea of the married state. His romantic platonism owed much, no doubt, to Shelley, but it was none the less a conception vital to the whole of his thought concerning human relationships and,

The Half-hearted Rebel

unlike some of his boyish borrowings from the 'Suntreader,' remained of lasting significance to him. For Browning, in his union with Elizabeth Barrett, was to live that very experience to which Shelley had restlessly aspired, but in vain. The nature of his early premonitions of this love is most clearly expressed in the second of the 'Queen Worship' series—'Cristina'—which tells of an adoration hopeless but triumphant, conceived in a flash of momentary recognition more significant for the 'I' of the poem than a lifetime of honours and ambition fulfilled:

> Doubt you if, in some such moment,
>   As she fixed me, she felt clearly,
> Ages past the soul existed,
>   Here an age 'tis resting merely,
> And hence fleets again for ages,
>   While the true end, sole and single,
> It stops here for is, this love-way,
>   With some other soul to mingle?
>
> Else it loses what it lived for,
>   And eternally must lose it . . .

The thought of a lovers' first meeting as in effect a 'dèja vu,' an earnest of some previous or extra-temporal existence, might seem merely fanciful, were it not to be fulfilled in the lives of Robert and Elizabeth Browning. But neither this poem nor 'In a Gondola,' the other love poem in his first book of lyrics, is on the high level of achievement of the rest. Clearly too much of what the poet longs for is still imaginative and imprecise. Yet the girl's song from the latter poem has an authenticity that immediately removes Browning from the ranks of the erotic dreamers. It has indeed a surprising sensuality, for Browning never accepted the nineteenth-century's dichotomy of flesh and spirit; it was a woman, not a fantasy of his own projection, that he sought, when he wrote:

> 'The moth's kiss, first!
> Kiss me as if you made believe
> You were not sure, this eve,
> How my face, your flower, had pursed
> Its petals up; so, here and there
> You brush it, till I grow aware
> Who wants me, and wide ope I burst.

William Sharp, one of the first of Browning's biographers, who knew him well in his old age, speaks of a number of early love affairs; one has certainly a feeling that his Paulines were no longer fictitious.

Of far greater accomplishment than these love poems, however, are two pieces in this same first book of lyrics which already establish Robert Browning in two fields which throughout his long life he never grew tired of exploring. The first is 'My Last Duchess,' a study in that vitality and unscrupulousness, that luxury and love of art, that cruelty and subtlety, he always associated with Italy and the Renaissance. The Middle Ages were outside the range of his understanding, since the idea of Catholic Christianity was entirely foreign to him. No poet was more Protestant in outlook. He was quick to sympathize with the victims of the Church's persecution; he saw the worldliness of its prelates and scorned its appeal to superstition; but its religious purpose and its ideal of moral government were outside his field of vision. He was therefore always at his happiest when writing of that age in which faith was overlaid with casuistry and mundane ambition. 'My Last Duchess' leads straight to 'The Bishop orders his Tomb in St. Praxed's Church,' published three years later. 'Artemis Prologizes,' his first

The Half-hearted Rebel

poem on a classical subject, opened for him a second field in which later he was to triumph, though it was followed by nothing more in this vein until his Greek translations of the seventies.

The publication of this little collection of lyrics denoted no weakening of Browning's dramatic ambitions; the poems were few and had been written at intervals over several years. His dearest wish was still to write for Macready a play which should have run at the Haymarket. The piece which came nearest to achieving this success, however, is perhaps the least individual of all his productions, *A Blot in the 'Scutcheon*, which would appear to have been written towards the end of 1841. It is a melodrama of no particular interest, artificial in its situations and even more undistinguished in its verse than *The Return of the Druses*. But its chief weakness lies in its author's sheer inability to construct a play or write dialogue. He was interested not in the clash of personalities, but in complexities of motive. His characters, therefore, when compelled to confront one another, habitually perform what might be called a soliloquy *à deux*. The play's third act opens with Tresham reflecting as he walks down the yew tree avenue towards the light in his sister's window, which is a signal to her lover. After thirty lines given over to his fears that she has disgraced the family name, he hears the midnight bell, and retires behind a tree to give place to a second soliloquist, his sister's lover, coming to keep his assignment and confide his plight to the audience in a mere sixteen lines.

Macready kept the play by him for two years, hoping to find some pretext for breaking his promise to stage it. Finally he decided to go ahead, though with no trust in its success. It was received with apparent favour by the first-night audience, but two very unfavourable reviews, one of which Browning suspected to have been inspired by Macready himself, gave the actor-manager the excuse for withdrawing *A Blot* after its third performance. 'Macready has used me vilely,' Browning wrote to Domett, and his friendship with Macready lapsed for twenty years from that day, after which interval they met again, each mourning for the loss of a wife, and were reconciled by mutual sympathy.

His next play, *Colombe's Birthday*, Browning submitted to Macready's rival at Covent Garden, Charles Kean, the son of that Edmund Kean whom he had so admired as a boy. Kean tried to keep the piece back for production in the next year, but Browning was impatient, and negotiations were broken off.

Colombe's Birthday is less artificial than *A Blot in the 'Scutcheon*. In its plot and its verse it makes fewer concessions to the low level of contemporary theatrical taste. The heroine, in fact, bears a slight resemblance to Pippa, while the hero voices Browning's conception of love as selfless sacrifice, which he had already sketched in 'Cristina'. But the play was not really conceived for the stage. Nor, indeed, was its successor, *Luria*, in which the poet returned to the historical manner of *The Return of the Druses*. It remained his favourite of all his attempts at drama, but no manager ever considered producing it. Certainly it made no concessions, either in subject or treatment, to the possibilities of a Haymarket or Drury Lane success. Browning felt free now, as he had not done in those plays which he had had hopes of seeing staged, to explore motive, to fill in background and to enrich the texture of his verse. *Luria* is set in fifteenth-century Italy, in Florence and in Pisa. It is a study in loyalty, in the loyalty of a Moorish mercenary general, whose character owes more than a little to Othello, and who is tempted by manifold incitements to treachery, but remains magnificently true to the city of his adoption, even when discredited. It is, of all Browning's plays, the only one that could conceivably be staged today.

His final drama, *A Soul's Tragedy*, is already half-way between a stage play and the internal drama of *Men and Women*. It is entirely concerned with motive, and with the unexpectednesses of human behaviour. Its setting is contemporary and Italian. The first act, in verse, tells of the poetry in the life of one Chiappino, who by a sudden act of heroism takes the blame for an assault on the Provost of a small town in the Papal states, committed by a friend, though partly at his instigation. But the friend's danger proves imaginary, and Chiappino in trying to prolong his heroic gesture becomes once more his old bombastic self; the second act, in prose, reduces the 'soul's tragedy,' if it could be dignified by such a term, to farce. For the Papal legate Ogniben is quite undisturbed by the action of either friend. 'I have known *Four* and twenty leaders of revolts,' he humorously concludes, adding one more to the '*Three* and twenty' he had claimed at his first entrance.

Browning made no further attempts at drama. But his experiments, unsuccessful though they had been, had served one good purpose. They had broken him of the obscurities of *Sordello*. The task of writing lines for Macready or Kean, and for actors whose comprehension was so limited that they supposed 'impeachment' to mean 'poaching,' had forced him to strive—not always successfully, it is true—for clarity even at the expense of writing lines almost entirely devoid of ore. So much he had gained from his otherwise almost fruitless endeavours.

In December 1840, a little before the publication of *Pippa Passes* and when the poet was twenty-eight, the

Browning family moved away from Camberwell, out into a large three-storeyed farmhouse at Hatcham, a Kentish village long since engulfed in the suburban spread of the city. From here he would take long walks out into the fields, preferably by night when from a neighbouring hill the lights of London could be seen glowing on the northern horizon, walks during which the lines of poems would begin to take shape in his head. In his upstairs study at Hatcham, in the blue shirt that he affected as his working dress, he toiled hopefully upon his plays; but at intervals between his dramatic endeavours and his social engagements he completed that larger batch of lyrical poems which came to him on his night walks, and which he published in 1845.

One cannot give any certain date to the separate poems among these *Dramatic Romances and Lyrics*, though most of them must have been composed during the three years before their publication. There are twenty-six of them, of which at least half a dozen advance, in their own particular genres, beyond the stage attained by the nearest corresponding poems in his earlier collection. 'How they Brought the Good News from Ghent to Aix,' with its persistent galloping rhythms, is more exciting, more graphic and more impetuous than any of the 'Cavalier Tunes' in the previous volume; and 'The Bishop orders his Tomb' carries the dramatic presentation of character and the imaginative reconstruction, not only of Renaissance detail but of a Renaissance attitude to life, considerably beyond the high-water mark of 'My Last Duchess.' Elizabeth Barrett wrote early in their correspondence that 'St. Praxed's' was the finest and most powerful of the poems he had given to Hood[1]—

[1] For 'Hood's Magazine', which was supported by various literary men during Hood's fatal illness.

The Half-hearted Rebel

'indeed full of the power of life. . . . and of death.' Ruskin—by a strange historical confusion—praised its marvellous apprehension of the medieval spirit. But in addition to its superscription, "Rome 15—", the signature of the Renaissance appears in every line. What could be less medieval than the pagan bishop's claim to have struck a most un-Christian bargain with his God.

> And have I not Saint Praxed's ear to pray
> Horses for ye, and brown Greek manuscripts,
> And mistresses with great smooth marbly limbs?

he asks his predatory 'nephews,' demanding only in return a tomb finer than 'Old Gandolf's,' in which he can

> lie through centuries
> And hear the blessed mutter of the mass,
> And see God made and eaten all day long,
> And feel the steady candle-flame and taste
> Good strong thick stupefying incense-smoke!

'St. Praxed's' is a chip struck from the hard stone of *Sordello*. But whilst in its setting the poem recalls Browning's most ambitious failure, the Bishop himself is a more highly coloured forerunner of Bishop Blougram, who was to make equally advantageous terms with his Maker. 'Well, here am I,' he concluded looking back on the comfortable grandeur of his life:

> Such were my gains, life bore this fruit to me,
> While writing all the same my articles
> On music, poetry, the fictile vase
> Found at Albano, chess, Anacreon's Greek . . .

There is little to distinguish these two bishops of the same church except their dates. In the same way the artist of 'Pictor Ignotus' looks forward to 'Andrea del Sarto' and to 'Fra Lippo Lippi. But though this piece also bore the century's date mark 15—, it was less a Renaissance picture than a timeless study in failure, reflecting in part Browning's own ill-success in finding applause and a public. Perhaps, concludes this unknown painter, conscious that his works might have obtained as much praise as a more fortunate rival's—perhaps they would have suffered too much if they had, at the hands of those who

> . . . buy and sell our pictures, take and give,
> Count them for garniture and household-stuff . . .

Soon, indeed, it is clear that Browning has put himself in the place of his character and that the gestures of the dealers and merchants were copied from those of nineteenth-century critics, whose prate he had been forced to listen to, and to whose daily pettiness *Sordello* and the plays had been exposed. So the unknown painter, returning to decorate

> These endless cloisters and eternal aisles
>   With the same series, Virgin, Babe and Saint,
> With the same cold calm beautiful regard . . .

consoled himself that at least no merchant trafficked with his heart. But Browning was now too buoyant and too vigorous a man to withdraw into the perfectionist seclusion of an artist content to forego his audience. 'Pictor Ignotus' was the expression of a mere passing mood.

Browning's first collection contained no poem written in the first person; in his rejection of *Pauline* he had turned against the voicing of sentiments which might be attributed to himself. In the new book, however, there are three pieces referring to particular situations and voicing private emotions. Yet so impersonal was

The Half-hearted Rebel

Robert Browning, so reticent and uncircumstantial about his statements, that even here, in 'Home Thoughts from Abroad,' in 'Home Thoughts from the Sea,' and in the lines to Nelson's memory which afterwards formed part of the poem 'Nationality in Drinks,' he seemed to speak with the almost anonymous voice of any man who thinks longingly of his country when away from it. In the same way he afterwards presented the picture in reverse, writing of his yearning for Italy when in England, in the poem 'De Gustibus.' Such a capacity for simple, unself-conscious emotion is the mark of a poet who has transcended the need to display himself.

'The Lost Leader,' on the other hand, another poem in this collection, while seeming to apply to an actual situation, is far from faithful to historical fact. For Wordsworth's abandonment of the liberal cause, or even Southey's, could hardly have been attributed to the temptations of 'a handful of silver' or any ribband to stick in a coat. Indeed Browning in his poetry seldom referred simply to contemporary events; nor did the day to day play of politics seriously interest him. When as in this poem, or in the more ambitious *Prince Hohenstiel-Schwangau*, he thought of certain living characters it was not the details or the rights and wrongs of their actions that interested him. He was concerned with their cast of mind, with their essential attitudes, rather than with the chance events of their lives, or their possible effect upon humanity.

Political partisanship played little part in Browning's character. He was certainly an advocate of the repeal of the Corn Laws; in his youth he had proclaimed himself a republican; but in his maturity, though he considered himself a liberal, he could not feel wholeheartedly, as could Elizabeth Barrett, on any subject less black and white than the principle of Italian unification. Human values always obtruded; he had at heart a contempt for politics. 'How exquisitely absurd,' he wrote to Elizabeth towards the end of his wooing, on the subject of Harriet Martineau's ambition to see women in Parliament—'how essentially retrograde a measure! Parliament seems no place for originating, creative minds—but for second-rate minds influenced by and bent on working out the results of these.'

For him the important issues lay on the plane neither of political action nor of supernatural religion, but on those of artistic creation and of love, those two of man's chief activities that seemed to him most closely allied; and nowhere did he express more explicitly the closeness of that relationship, as he saw it, than in the poem 'Saul,' the first nine sections of which appeared in his 1845 collection. It is not, however, till the end of the poem, which was not written till later, that the full significance of David's song emerges. Not till then is it clear that for him, as for Robert Browning his creator, the out-pouring of love in song, the embodiment of emotion in a created thing, leads to an acceptance at a deeper level of insight of the reality of God, not as a supernatural presence, but in his Jewish and Protestant aspect as the supreme lawgiver.

> I have gone the whole round of creation: I saw and I spoke:
> I, a work of God's hand for that purpose, received in my brain
> And pronounced on the rest of his handwork—returned him again
> His creation's approval or censure: I spoke as I saw:
> I report, as a man may of God's work—all's love, yet all's law.

The song is concluded, the king healed and the shep-

The Half-hearted Rebel

herd boy yearns to pour out for his father—for so Saul seems to him—love beyond the possibilities of earthly love. It is in this complete self-abnegation that to the two components love and song is added that *tertium quid*, the revelation of divine significance. The theme of 'Saul' is central to the whole body of Browning's work, and to his faith in a supernatural reality, not elsewhere and afterwards, but here and immanent in man's two most profound emotions—that are in a sense one—his love and his powers of creation.

While 'Saul,' in its final version at least, flows up from the depths of that understanding of Browning's which is so often and so easily dismissed as a mere superficial optimism, a facile belief in material comfort and automatic progress, another poem which was still incomplete when published in his 1845 collection, speaks more profoundly and less fancifully than 'Cristina' of the force of selfless love which Browning hoped to find in himself when the occasion should call it out. 'The Flight of the Duchess,' however, comes from a deeper level of the imagination than 'Cristina,' from a level indeed in which the poet understood the dangers of duality, of the cleavage between body and spirit and between mind and its object. 'The Flight of the Duchess' had been prompted by the sudden recollection of a song which the poet had heard as a child sung by a gipsy woman one Guy Fawkes day. The poem immediately establishes an atmosphere much more akin to that in which Childe Roland was later to ride than to the imaginary country over which Cristina reigned. 'Following the queen of the Gipsies O' had been the song's simple refrain, but the land of the gipsies the poem conjured up presented, as it had done to the child, a double picture; it was the country of magic both black and white.

Yet for all its half-symbolic, dreamlike opening the poem had, in the half-finished state in which it first appeared, what amounted to a social moral. The Duchess was a pampered Victorian bride, a Pippa, perhaps, trapped into conventional marriage and watched over on the sly by the Duke's witch of a mother. It was not until several months later that a chance remark by a friend, whom Browning had met staying away in Flintshire, set the poem working again. It was Kinglake, the author of *Eothen*, who remarked on that September morning that 'the deer had already begun to break the ice in the pond,' and his words were incorporated in the poem, at the very point where it had been broken off:

> Well, early in autumn, at first winter-warning,
> When the stag had to break with his foot, of a
>   morning,
> A drinking hole out of the fresh tender ice
> That covered the pond . . .

The message of 'The Flight of the Duchess,' as it was completed, is entirely a symbolic one; the social moral slips away into oblivion. For the poem was, in essence, the product of an unnoticed day dream, that twice required the stimulus of a magic and suggestive phrase to bring it to consciousness, and such fantasy can, at times, speak more truly of a man's deep experience than do tales or reasonings that have undergone a more vigorous intellectual sifting.

The landscape of 'The Flight of the Duchess' is neither Italian, nor German, nor English; it is a nightmare country of dualities whose contrasting halves are alike ruled over by the petty Duke. Its nature is described by the huntsman who finally contrives the Duchess's escape from it.

The Half-hearted Rebel

Ours is a great wild country:
   If you climb to our castle's top,
   I don't see where your eye can stop;
For when you've passed the cornfield country,
Where vineyards leave off, flocks are packed,
And sheep-range leads to cattle-tract,
And cattle-tract to open-chase,
And open-chase to the very base
Of the mountain where, at a funeral pace,
Round about, solemn and slow,
One by one, row after row,
Up and up the pine-trees go,
So, like black priests up, and so,
Down the other side again
   To another greater, wilder country,
That's one vast red drear burnt-up plain,
Branched through and through with many a vein
Whence iron's dug, and copper's dealt;
   Look right, look left, look straight before,—
Beneath they mine, above they smelt,
   Copper-ore and iron-ore,
And forge and furnace mould and melt,
   And so on, more and ever more,
Till at the last, for a bounding belt,
   Comes the salt sand hoar of the great sea-shore,
—And the whole is our Duke's country.

Not only was the Duke's country, itself a protagonist in the drama, divided into two contrasting halves, agricultural and industrial, but the Duke himself was the son of parents coming from opposite worlds, the good old Duke and his sick, tall, yellow Duchess, who was 'the daughter of God knows who;' and if the Duke had running in his veins the blood of nobility and of some unknown tribe, he partook also of another duality. He was the twin, though not by parentage, of the huntsman, the Duchess's silent and faithful lover. For was not this narrator of the poem his *alter ego*, 'born the day this present Duke was?' But the dualism of the poem goes even further. The sick tall Duchess and the queen of the gipsies, who are the evil and the good geniuses of the poem's Pippa-like heroine, are again contradictory aspects of the same figure. It is hardly strange indeed that Mrs. Sutherland Orr in her *Handbook to Robert Browning's Works* pronounces the poem to be, like Childe Roland, 'incompatible with rational explanation and independent of it.' For it is concerned with contradictions of personality at a very deep level, and its symbolism is only explicable in psychological terms.

The poem was in the first place intended to tell 'of the life the lady was to lead with her future gipsy lover, a *real* life'; so Browning spoke of the poem to Elizabeth Barrett. But in the end he 'wrote it anyhow, just to get it done.' But this is only a rational explanation of the poem's refusal to take an intellectual shape at variance with the poet's own profoundest experience. The Duchess, who embodied his own powers of love and creation—untried powers of which he was by no means certain—must be led by the good huntsman, away from his brother, the wicked—or perhaps only stupid—Duke, out of the land of worldly contradictions into the land of pure poetry, the land of the gipsies, who know 'How love is the only good in the world.' The gipsies represent the secret watchers, the powers that lie dormant in the depths of our minds capable of guiding us out of the labyrinth of conflicting desires—which is the Duke's world of our own restless lives. 'We,' says the gipsy queen, 'pursue thy whole career.' But to bring the Duchess to her gipsy lover, to carry his symbolism to the point of reconciliation, where the two rival worlds become one, would have overtaxed the poet's experi-

The Half-hearted Rebel

ence. All he could do was to tell of her escape, of the selfless love of the huntsman who contrived it, of the gipsy queen's prophecy concerning the probation and fulfilment that awaited her in the land of white magic, and of the protection that the gipsies could give her in this world.

> Whether it be thy lot to go,
> For the good of us all, where the haters meet
> In the crowded city's horrible street;
> Or thou step alone through the morass
> Where never sound yet was
> Save the dry quick clap of the stork's bill,
> For the air is still and the water still,
> When the blue breast of the dipping coot
> Dives under, and all is mute.
> So, at the last shall come old age,
> Decrepit as befits that stage;
> How else wouldst thou retire apart
> With the hoarded memories of thy heart,
> And gather all to the very least
> Of the fragments of life's earlier feast,
> Let fall through eagerness to find
> The crowning dainties yet behind?
> Ponder on the entire past
> Laid together thus at last,
> When the twilight helps to fuse
> The first fresh with the faded hues,
> And the outline of the whole,
> As round eve's shades their framework roll,
> Grandly fronts for once thy soul.

'The Flight of the Duchess' was in its inception a poem of escape, a charm against the powers of death wielded by the strange Guy Fawkes Day gipsy, with her unearthly song. But it is more than that. It is the complement of 'Saul.' For whereas in that poem Browning attains an assurance of the reality of a divine law, in 'The Flight of the Duchess' he conjures up a picture of a life under magic protectors, that shall lead up, as he himself attempted to when he wrote his *Parleyings*, to a comprehension before death of 'the outline of the whole.' Both poems are concerned with the resolution of duality by the powers of love and creation, but only in 'The Flight of the Duchess' is the cleft nature of the world of experience symbolically stated.

Technically, this poem is in the descent rather from 'The Pied Piper' than from any other piece in the earlier book. Elizabeth Barrett praised it for its 'perfect rhymes, perfectly new and all clashing together as by natural attraction.' But clearly she was a little puzzled by what she called its novelty. It is possible that she did not see how much, like 'The Pied Piper,' it owed to Hood and to Barham. At its weakest indeed, it degenerates into the pure Ingoldsby of such lines as:

In brief, my friend, set all the devils in hell free
And turn them out to carouse in a belfry
And treat the priests to a fifty part canon,
And then you may guess how that tongue of his ran on.

Elizabeth returned to the poem twice, in later letters, concluding on the first occasion that its rhythm answered to Browning's own description of 'speech half asleep or song half awake'—a phrase more applicable to the poem's inspiration than to its texture. But reverting once again to the novelty of its rhythms she decided on the second occasion that it was 'something like (if like anything) what the Greeks called pedestrian metre . . . between metre and prose . . . the difficult rhymes combining too quite curiously with the easy looseness of the general measure.' Browning's own statement that he had

The Half-hearted Rebel

written it anyhow, to get it done, throws rather more light on the reasons for the poem's uneveness. Its symbolism was clearly intractable to the surface intellect, and so it had to be left in an unpolished state, still bearing the mark of technical influences not wholly absorbed. It is however a poem of very much greater intensity than 'The Pied Piper,' and with 'Saul' and *Pippa* stood at the summit of Robert Browning's achievement at the moment of his first meeting with Elizabeth Barrett.

Chapter Three

ALLIANCE OF POETS

'IT is quite startling,' wrote Elizabeth Barrett, three months after her first meeting with Robert Browning, 'quite startling and humiliating, to observe how you combine such large tracts of experience of outer and inner life, of books and men, of the world and the arts of it; curious knowledge as well as general knowledge . . . and deep thinking as well as wide acquisition . . . and you, looking none the older for it all!—yes, and being besides a man of genius and working your faculty and not wasting yourself over a surface or away from an end?' Such was the impression of single-mindedness that Robert Browning made, at thirty-three, upon a woman who by the confined nature of her semi-invalid life had become an acute and ready observer of the few visitors who were admitted to her room. She saw herself as one who could expect nothing more from her active existence, as one who must live through her writing and, vicariously, through the men and women who were her friends. But she found herself outmatched in subtlety by this outwardly fashionable young man whose face betrayed none of the experience vouched for by his poetry and his conversation. 'Read me no more backwards,' she had protested two months before, 'with your Hebrew, putting in your own vowel points without my leave.' He was subtle, yet in a curious way undecided, over-diffident, and unwilling to trust his own judgment. 'You persist in making me choose the days,' she grumbled, having made it amply clear that his visits were always welcome to her. 'It is not for me to do it, but for you.'

She found him still divided in mind over the kind of poetry he wanted to write. On the one side he had not given up his ambition to explore further the vein of romantic self-dramatization opened up in those three 'sadly imperfect demonstrations of even mere ability,' to quote his own denigratory verdict, *Pauline*, *Paracelsus* and *Sordello*. He was conscious of great powers of creation within him, but far from certain in what direction they would take him. 'What I have printed gives no knowledge of me,' he had written to Elizabeth Barrett before they met. 'It evidences abilities of various kinds, if you will . . . that I think. But I never have begun, even, what I hope I was born to begin and end—R. B. a poem.' Was it, however, an autobiographical poem that lay within him still unexpressed, or was it that his life had so far failed to take sufficient shape? Certainly he was disappointed with his work and spoke of meaning to begin afresh in deep earnest and without affectation. There is no wilful affectation about any of those first poems, except perhaps *Pauline*; his attitudinizing was no more than the mark of his continued immaturity. Nor were they lacking in earnestness. His long pre-occupation with the theatre had certainly led him to write pieces in which any deep seriousness would have been out of place. But even his plays were never trivial. These strictures upon his work were no more than reflections of a deep sense of unfulfilment. He had reached the age of thirty-two without undergoing any vital experience, and harboured still in the depths of his heart an unacknowledged guilt for the half-rebellion of his boyhood, and for the betrayal of the Shelleyan ideal that its collapse had entailed. His friendships and embryonic love affairs had been weakened by the strength and intimacy of his relationship with his parents. He saw the security of his childhood as a precious asset, yet felt that the very firmness of his early hold on life justified—perhaps almost required of him—some undefined but drastic step that might imperil the whole of his future happiness. He was ready for action, he knew not of what kind—for, the past being 'gained, secure and on record,' he was confident that nothing now could 'lose him his life,' even if he were to make a clean break with the 'old days.' For the 'old days' had left one adult side of his nature unsatisfied. We have already seen that his sociability was no more than an outward show, that he visited and entertained his friends more through fear that some 'unknown god'—or goddess—might escape him if he did not, than for the pleasure he took in company; 'I never was without good, kind, generous friends and lovers,' he wrote to Elizabeth many months before they met. 'Perhaps they came at the wrong time—I never wanted them . . . I never deceived myself much, nor called my feelings for people other than they were.' He was prepared, so early, to trust her with the deep knowledge he had acquired of his own character. In casual relationships prone to pose, he treated Elizabeth from the outset with a confessional candour that was called out in him by the rapid maturing of their friendship. It was as if they had known each other before. Preliminary formalities yielded almost immediately to intimate discussion, which was facilitated by the half-illusion that it was their poetry and not their private concerns they were speaking of. But already in his second letter Browning was voicing his self-dissatis-

Alliance of Poets

faction, though under the guise of anatomizing his failure to write the poetry he wished to. 'You speak out,' he pronounced. 'I only make men and women speak— give you truth broken into prismatic hues, and fear the pure white light, even if it is in me.' Here, perhaps, he was indicating his reasons for not having written 'R. B., a poem'—that his self-knowledge, acute though it was, remained insufficient, or that he was afraid of it. 'But I am going to try,' he went on; 'so it will be no small comfort to have your company just now, seeing that when you have your men and women aforesaid, you are buried with them, whereas it seems bleak, melancholy work, this talking to the wind (for I have begun)— yet I don't think I shall let *you* hear, after all, the savage things about Popes and imaginative religions that I must say.'

The letter would suggest that Browning was then at work on some early and less tolerant versions of *Christmas Eve and Easter Day*, which were not formally written and published till some five years later. A few weeks afterwards when Elizabeth told him something of a modern poem she was contemplating, he reverted to this subject of speaking out. 'The poem you propose to make for the times,' he says, 'is the *only* poem to be undertaken now by you or anyone that *is* a poet at all; the only reality, only effective piece of service to be rendered God and man; it is what I have been all my life intending to do and now shall be much, much nearer doing, since you will be along with me.' On February 26th 1845, the first day of that spring in the course of which, they both hoped, a meeting between them might be possible, he had taken leave once more of his dramatic ambitions. *Luria* should be his last play: 'there can no good come,' he concluded, 'of keeping this wild company any longer.'

Not only were the plays to be dismissed, however, but he was to abandon too the vein of poetry that he had worked to such advantage in his first collection of lyrics and in its successor, now almost ready for the printer. 'These got rid of,' he said of *Luria* and *A Soul's Tragedy*, 'I will do as you bid me and—say first I have some Romances and Lyrics, all dramatic to dispatch, and *then*, I shall stoop of a sudden under and out of this dancing ring of men and women hand in hand, and stand still awhile, should my eyes dazzle, and when that's over, they will be gone and you will be there, *pas vrai*? For, as I think I told you, I always shiver involuntarily when I look—no, glance—at this First Poem of mine to be.'

If it was indeed to be no more than 'a tract for the times,' R. B. a poem took eventual shape as *Christmas Eve and Easter Day*; but if, as the importance he attached to it seemed to convey, Browning was then envisaging a more intimate self-confession, this proposed great work remained unwritten. For seldom in his maturity did he abandon the dramatic method, the presentation of a facet of the truth reflected in the mind of a character chosen for the purpose; and when in his declining years he attempted in *Fifine at the Fair* and *La Saisiaz* to speak directly of his own deepest experience it eluded him. 'They will be gone, and you will be there,' was capable of another construction, and a profounder one, if transferred from the context of poetry into that of the life experience from which the poetry came. 'They' stood not for a class of seemingly objective lyrics, but rather for inner limitations, for the failure to meet with equal friendship offers of affection made in the past, for the last trammels of childhood dependence which, with all his confidence that their severance would not lose him his life, did still prevent his making a break with the old

Alliance of Poets

days. His quickly ripening love for Elizabeth Barrett was in itself that masterpiece which he had seen as his 'First Poem.' In 'Saul' he had expressed the intimate connection he had discovered between love and poetry, and the religious certainty born of the release of their joint powers; in 'The Flight of the Duchess' he had glimpsed that other, gipsy country—represented on earth perhaps by Italy—in which life could be freed from the rack of duality; in *Pippa* he had drawn a symbol of that innocence and womanly compassion—*das Ewig-Weibliche*—that could lead him to it. For only when seen with the eyes of Pippa, of the Duchess, and later of Pompilia in *The Ring and the Book*, could the humdrum shabbiness of everyday existence, the crimes, the meannesses and failures to keep faith—which he saw without him, and reproached himself for finding within him—be redeemed. Now in a supreme human relationship he was to experience that rare ripening into maturity which of the Romantics only Keats had known—and which Keats had discovered only when confronted by imminent and seemingly premature death. From this experience, and from the loss of his wife, which did not bring it to an end, was to be born the greatest of Browning's poetry. But in the year and a half of his wooing he wrote very little indeed.

From his first letter, complimentary, and exploratory at the same time of the possibilities of a meeting, to that first meeting four months later, between an apparently chronic invalid of thirty-nine, and a young man some six years her junior, their intimacy grew rapidly. For both from the outset gave themselves unreservedly to the relationship. Despite Robert Browning's surface timidity, his diffidence in the matter of fixing dates and his repeated apologies for having possibly overtired a woman to whom he was bringing the breath of life, it was to his preconceived pattern that events quite rapidly shaped themselves. For as the huntsman released the Duchess, or as Perseus, in a favourite picture upon Robert Browning senior's walls, released Andromeda, so the poet was preparing himself for that elopement which to Elizabeth Barrett and to her friends would have seemed at the outset beyond her physical capacities. But Browning knew—or acted as if he knew—that his first letter was the beginning of something richer with promise than a mere literary acquaintanceship. 'I do, as I say, love these books, with all my heart,' he wrote of her poetry, 'and I love you too.' It is easy to miss the unexpected ring in these words, now that one is so familiar with the course of events to which they were a prelude. Yet if he was the shaper of this partnership, she fell readily enough into her role, however unsuitable it might then seem to one 'scarcely to be called young now,' as she expressed it. But whereas her age and her invalidism—based certainly on some pulmonary weakness—made her renunciation of any thought of marriage not unreasonable, Browning's initial assumption of a similar resignation is extremely hard to explain. 'Being no longer in the first freshness of life,' he wrote to her in the autumn of 1845, when he had begun to envisage their eventual marriage, 'and having for many years now made up my mind to the impossibility of loving any woman . . . having wondered at this in the beginning, and fought not a little against it, having acquiesced in it at last, and accounted for it all to myself, and become, if anything, rather proud of it than sorry,' he had till then, he claimed 'a mind set in ultimate order, so I fancied, for the few years more.' This was not a mere self-dramatization, a spontaneous reaction to her statement that there were obstacles, though not the financial or paternal obstacles

Alliance of Poets

that he had supposed, to her giving him the prize, the last and best of all. It was a revelation rather of the cleft between Robert Browning's inner conviction which had guided him to Wimpole Street, and an outer affectation of despair which had so far impeded his approach to his fellow men. 'I have made myself almost ridiculous,' he wrote at a still later date, 'by a kind of male prudery with respect to young ladies . . . I was very little inclined to get involved in troubles and troubles for nothing at all. And as for marrying . . .' Perhaps he exaggerated his former restraint and timidity; such early lyrics as 'The Moth's Kiss First' . . . suggest that he did. But chief among the contradictions that are mirrored in 'The Flight of the Duchess' was that between the line of his fate and the line of his intellectual imagination.

Imaginatively, throughout his poetry, he was apt to construct false solutions to his problems. In 'The Flight' he had wished to describe the gipsy country, but had been unable; in *Christmas Eve and Easter Day* he was to build a precarious literary superstructure upon the sound but lowly base of his experience. But in his love for Elizabeth Barrett the imaginative prevision and the ripening of the relationship were as one. Their love was, it must be repeated, the masterpiece he had foreseen. The relative parts played in his life and his writing by the rival forces of heart and head, of inspiration and invention, are clearly revealed in yet another letter to Elizabeth Barrett. 'One should study the mechanical part of the art, as nearly all that there is to be studied,' he wrote, 'for the more one sits and thinks over the creative process, the more it confirms itself as "inspiration," nothing more nor less. Or, at worst, you write down old inspirations, what you remember of them . . .

but with *that* it begins. "Reflection" is exactly what it names itself—a re-presentation, in scattered rays from every angle of incidence, of what first of all became present in a great light, a whole one! So tell me how these lights are born, if you can! But I can tell anybody how to make melodious verses.' He had, he confessed, been at one time impatient of his technique, of his music, and anxious to catch the inspiration nearer its source. As a poet he distrusted the intellectual processes. In his life, hitherto, he had given them too much exercise; a great deal of the self-knowledge of which he boasted was no more than hair-splitting introspection. Nor in his poems did he always draw on deep sources. 'So far differently was I circumstanced of old,' he wrote in this same letter of June 14th 1845, 'that I used rather to go about for a subject of offence to people, writing ugly things in order to warn the ungenial and timorous off my grounds at once.' Such was no doubt the genesis of the 'Soliloquy in the Spanish Cloister,' and perhaps of the two 'Madhouse Cells' as well. But these poems could not have been as successful as they were, had it not been for the residue of nightmare self-reproach which lay at almost as deep a level within him as the purer spring of inspiration.

On another occasion, enlarging on the strange story of the writing of 'The Flight of the Duchess,' Browning revealed with even greater clarity the relative parts played in the conception of his poems by the intellectual plan and the uprush of inspiration. 'It is an odd fact,' he wrote on the subject of the now completed poem, 'yet characteristic of my accomplishings one and all in this kind, that of the poem, the real conception of an evening (two years ago fully), of *that*, not a line is written—though perhaps after all, what I am going to call the accessories in the story are real though indirect reflexes of the original idea, and so supersede properly enough the necessity of its personal appearance, so to speak. But, as I conceived the poem, it consisted entirely of the gipsy's description of the life the lady was to lead with her future gipsy lover—a *real* life, not an unreal one like that with the Duke. And as I meant to write it, all their wild adventures would have come out and the insignificance of the former vegetation have been deducible only—as the main subject has become now . . .' 'You are more faithful to your first *idea* than to your first *plan*,' was Elizabeth Barrett's shrewd comment.

The early love letters contain many such workshop secrets, for it was, ostensibly at least, as fellow craftsmen that they had come together. But discussions of inspiration and technique led easily to more intimate exchanges of confidences, and from there to mutual confessions of the value each found in the other, and to the mutual concern of each for the other's health and happiness. One can see Elizabeth Barrett's initial alarm at the emotional demands their relationship made of her, and her almost angry insistence that he should remain, as at the inception, the more responsible partner. He was too prone to talk of his 'real inferiority' to herself, and to indulge in over-wordy self-depreciation. 'For every poor spark of a Vesuvius or Stromboli in my microcosm,' he proclaimed, 'there are huge layers of ice and pits of black cold water.' His protestations that he would wish to serve her—as the huntsman had served the Duchess in the poem—without hope of reward, brought from her the sharp expostulation that the offer might be 'generous in you—but in me, where were the integrity?' But for her health, she assured him, she would accept the trust with which he honoured her. And when her fears diminished, and she began to envisage the abandoning of her recluse's life, which she had no doubt adopted, in part at least, in order to protect herself from just such demands as he now made, then her health began to improve. She who had once been exhausted by a half-hour's visit, was able to walk out, to drive out, and to face the prospect of married life on moderate means, very largely hers. For she had a small inherited income, and he little or nothing of his own.

In the spring and summer of their first meetings Robert Browning was finishing the two plays *Luria* and *A Soul's Tragedy*. Then, after many months of apparent idleness, perhaps broken by work on his poem attacking Popes and imaginative religions, he proposed during the next summer, that of 1846, to write 'one last poem . . . a poem to publish or not to publish; but a proper introduction to the afterwork.' For now, he told Elizabeth, his poetry was far from being the completest expression of his being. 'I hate to refer to it,' he wrote, 'or I could tell you why, wherefore . . . *prove* how imperfect . . . how unsatisfactory it must of necessity be. Still, I should not much object, if, such as it is, it were the best, the flower of my life . . . but that is all to come, and through you, mainly, or more certainly.' Browning's dissatisfaction with his work hitherto was excessive; in effect there was no clean break between *Pippa* and the 'afterwork,' the great poetry written during the years of their marriage, between 'The Tomb at St. Praxed's' and 'Fra Lippo Lippi,' or between 'My Last Duchess' and 'The Statue and the Bust.' In 'Christmas Eve' and in 'Easter Day,' however, he very deliberately strayed from the main path of his development in an endeavour to define his religious position. This costly failure was, perhaps, the result of his future wife's influence. Indeed the religious position he did define was very close to her own as she had set it down for him in a letter in August 1846. But there is no mention in their correspondence of any new poem actually begun, only of the completion of projects in hand. She in fact encouraged his idleness. For frequently in his letters he complained of headaches and unspecified minor ailments for which Elizabeth could see a certain cure in more walking and less working. So though her admiration of his poems reinforced his belief in his own powers, the immediate effect of their year and a half's wooing was to take him from his work. Indeed, his first publication after the two plays, the small book containing 'Christmas Eve' and 'Easter Day,' did not appear till the end of a four years' silence, in 1850.

The correspondence, though rich during its early months in discussions of poetry and in mutual revelations of character and beliefs, narrows as it proceeds. Soon both were almost exclusively preoccupied with the growth and nature of their love, with arrangements for meetings and with precautions against detection. Their intimacy moved steadily towards a marriage, overcoming obstacles which proved, one after another, imaginary. Her fears of perpetual invalidism, his diffidences, and the menace of her father's interference were less strong than a certainty existing in them both that their relationship was the product of some power stronger than themselves. 'Nothing is my work,' Elizabeth proclaimed. 'Let it be God's work and yours . . . indeed I exclaim to myself about the miracle of it far more even than you can do. It seems to me still a dream how you came here at all . . . the very machinery of it seems miraculous. Why did I receive you and only you? Can I tell? no, not a word.' This is not mere lovers' hyperbole; it is a clear-sighted astonishment that something so unexpected and yet so inevitable could have taken place.

The elopement of Robert Browning and Elizabeth Barrett has been so often described that it can here be briefly passed over. To obtain Mr. Barrett's permission would have been for ever impossible, and in September 1846 he was about to remove his family into the country, while No. 60 Wimpole Street was being painted. This precipitated an arrangement that had been discussed in a flurry of letters which the lovers exchanged by every post. 'I will do as you wish—understand,' was the final form of her consent, in the postscript to a note announcing the migration from London. 'Saturday, Septr. 12. 1846 $\frac{1}{4}11—11\frac{1}{4}$ a.m. (91),' Browning scribbled on the envelope of a letter that had reached him that morning, the last that Elizabeth Barrett wrote before the wedding, which took place in Marylebone Church at that hour and on that day, on the ninety-first of their meetings. Only Miss Barrett's maid was admitted to the secret—such was their fear of Mr. Barrett's reprisals against any member of the family whom they might take into their confidence. Elizabeth returned to Wimpole Street for another week whilst packing and final preparations were completed. During this time Browning did not care to call, since that would necessitate his asking for his wife under her maiden name. This did not prevent a daily exchange of letters, concerning the departure of steamships for the continent, and the exact form of the wedding notice that would be inserted in the papers on their departure. 'Robert Browning Esquire, of New Cross, author of *Paracelsus*, to Elizabeth Barrett, eldest daughter of Edward Moulton Barrett Esquire of Wimpole Street. Would you put it so?' she asked, half guessing that he would demur at the mention of *Paracelsus*. 'So the advertisement shall run,' he replied, 'save and except the avowal of *Paracelsus.*'

The Barrett's departure for a house near Leatherhead was announced for the following Monday, which precipitated the elopement, perhaps by some days. Browning was confusing himself over the times and dates of trains, muddling departures from Southampton with departures from Havre. In the final arrangements Elizabeth seems to have been the more practical of the partners.

In the afternoon of September 19th Elizabeth Barrett Browning stole out of No. 60 Wimpole Street attended by her maid and her dog, while the family were at dinner. Unobserved they walked to Hodgson's the booksellers in Great Marylebone Street, where Robert Browning was waiting. The boxes had been sent ahead, and in a cab they departed for Nine Elms station to catch the five o'clock train for Southampton, and a new life.

From Southampton, by way of Havre to Paris. Then through Orleans, and Avignon to Marseilles, whence by ship to Leghorn and from there to Pisa. The news of the marriage caused some stir in England; for an elopement was an exciting event even though neither of the pair was a romantic or well-known figure. 'So Robert Browning and Miss Barrett have gone off together,' commented the aged Wordsworth. 'I hope they can understand each other. Nobody else can.' 'My daughter should have been thinking of another world,' is the only recorded comment of the bride's father. But there were many well-wishers: Browning's family; Mr. Kenyon, through whose introduction the couple had originally met, and Thomas Carlyle who wrote that 'if ever there was a union indicated by the finger of Heaven itself . . . it seemed to me . . . to be this.'

Browning had paid a second visit to Italy in the summer of 1844, before the beginning of their correspondence, and found there the same freedom and inspiration he had discovered on his first visit. Already Elizabeth had contemplated a stay in Italy for the benefit of her health. But Browning had first investigated possibilities of work in London; he had even contemplated a post in the reading room of the British Museum. Later, when he was already in Italy, he offered himself, though more out of political sympathy than for the salary he would gain, as secretary to the Embassy which he expected to be opened at Rome. But no minister was appointed; and hopes of Italy's unity were deferred. The cause of Italy was already dear to both the Brownings; to Elizabeth it was an uncritical enthusiasm, but Robert's feelings were not always on the fervent level of his 'Italian in England.' Originally they had planned only to spend the winter abroad. The implacability of Mr. Barrett, however, who refused so much as to open his daughter's letters, persuaded them to stay, and prolong a visit to Florence into a permanent residence there. The small English and American colony in the city welcomed them, and the sociable side of Browning's nature responded to a few new and admiring friends, but for the most part they remained at home, working and rejoicing in each other's company. Elizabeth's small income, left to her by an uncle, and some money which Browning received from home enabled them to exist modestly, though far from uncomfortably. 'In Florence,' wrote Elizabeth, 'for three hundred a year one may live much like the Grand Duchess, and go to the opera in the evening at five pence halfpenny.' Her own health sufficiently improved for her to make long sight-seeing expeditions, riding even, on one occasion, in an unsprung carriage along a rough and stony road to a monastery in the Appenines. There Browning was welcomed and allowed to play on the organ of the monastery chapel, upon which Milton was believed to have played two hundred years before. Elizabeth, however, found the Abbot reluctant to entertain a lady, and after five days the pair of English poets departed.

The incident clearly demonstrates Browning's faint comprehension of the Catholic attitude. For despite his frequent choice of Catholic subjects for many of his greatest poems, he had hardly even an average outsider's understanding of Catholicism. No doubt he thought it most unreasonable of the Abbot to turn his wife away. He behaved, unintentionally no doubt, throughout his residence in Italy as if he were living in a Protestant country, whose native rite was no more than an archaic and local anachronism. Perhaps he was encouraged in this attitude by the example of 'Father Prout,' an eccentric and entertaining Irish Jesuit whose true name was Francis Mahony. Browning had met him for the first time at some London dinner table, and Prout was the first person he bumped into when he arrived at Leghorn on his wedding journey. Later, in Florence, the Jesuit turned up at a moment when Elizabeth had an attack of fever and, to the horror of the Italian servant, mixed with his own hands a potion of eggs and port wine, which he persuaded her to drink. This remarkable man was a contributor to *Fraser's Magazine*, and during Pio Nono's short-lived liberal phase acted as Rome correspondent for the radical *Daily News*. His journalistic activities were said to have ruined his hopes of preferment, and he now wandered, with seeming aimlessness, from Florence to Rome and from Rome to Paris, greeting and gossiping with any English families who happened to be travelling. 'A very singular person,' Elizabeth Browning wrote of him, perhaps a little guardedly, 'of whom the world tells a thousand and one tales, you know. But of whom I shall speak as I find him. Not very refined in a social sense by any manner of means,' she went on, 'but a most accomplished scholar—having seen all the ends of the earth and the men thereof, and possessing the art of talk and quotation to an amusing degree.' A few weeks later she was giving her sister a more circumstantial account of this 'unrefined' priest. 'And now, will you all believe that Father Prout has spent *every evening here except one* since I wrote last! . . . he is our man of the mountain . . . and we think it a decided gain whenever we can get tea over before he comes and fixes himself at his smoking post for three hours at least. As a matter of course the wine is rung for instantly, with an apparatus for spitting! . . . Poor Robert has been sorely taxed between his good nature and detestation of the whole proceeding.' But 'one likes the human nature of the man,' she concludes. There can certainly be no doubt that this eccentric worldling served, on his over frequent visits, as a model for the pictures Browning was later to draw of Catholic priests. There is certainly something of Prout in such a successor to St. Praxed's most scandalous bishop as the intellectual temporizer Blougram.

In 'Christmas Eve' and 'Easter Day,' Browning attempted to present a picture of Catholicism as a picturesque survival, not entirely dead at heart. There, in imagination, he penetrates to the centre of that faith, and views the basilica of St. Peter's alive with worshippers during the Christmas Eve service; its chancel body and nave so overcrowded that men are perched on the tombs and the statues,

> All famishing in expectation
> Of the main-altar's consummation.

But the poet and narrator remains outside, hesitating on the threshold stone, and watches the figure of Christ, whom he has been following, enter there too—as earlier He had entered into a dissenting house, and as afterwards He will enter the Göttingen lecture hall of a 'hawk-nosed, high-cheek-boned' professor—because

> Their faith's heart beats, though her head swims
> Too giddily to guide her limbs,
> Disabled by their palsy-stroke
> From propping mine.

'Christmas Eve' and 'Easter Day,' though intended as separate poems, must be considered together as marking two stages in a single quest for religious certainty. As a whole they are a failure, for their argument is flat and discursive, their imagery dead, and their verse a loose shamble. But there are moments when they flare up with the harsh light of vision, reminiscent of that light which played over the Duke's wild country in 'The Flight of the Duchess.' Such moments provide the only beauties in that long-pondered poem, in which he had proposed to put aside his men and women and speak out, as Elizabeth did. For it was her aim to write poetry which would 'rush into the drawing-rooms and the like, meeting face to face the Humanity of the Age, and speaking the truth as I conceive it out plainly.' 'Christmas Eve' is devoted to corporate religion, 'Easter Day' to the spiritual life of the individual; in both Browning examines the three alternative creeds competing for the souls of his contemporaries: the Nonconformity of his youth; Catholicism, which was just beginning to make the first of its spectacular conversions, and a dilute ethical Christianity based on the free criticism of the Bible. This last, which shook the faith of Arthur Hugh Clough and with which Matthew Arnold struck his compromise, was for Browning even less tempting than Catholicism; yet in the exhausted air of the Bible-critic's lecture-hall too, there dwelt, he admitted, something to find an echo in the Christian soul.

His own choice—or his wife's which for the moment he adopted as his—remained an etiolated version of that Nonconformity from which he had once half-heartedly rebelled, and of which he gives an acid picture in the chapel description with which 'Christmas Eve' opens. For, despite the preaching man's immense stupidity as he 'poured his doctrine forth, full measure'—certainly a childhood memory—Browning found here the true spring 'welling up from underground,' even if 'mingled with the taints of earth.' Therefore, he tepidly decided, here was the message nearest to that gospel of love that he had stated at white heat in 'Saul'. For

> God who registers the cup
>   Of mere cold water, for his sake
> To a disciple rendered up,
>   Disdains not his own thirst to slake
> At the poorest love was ever offered.

If the poem did not rise above such pedestrian Sunday-school moral-mongering, it could be dismissed out of hand as a mere unfortunate attempt to write in a manner foreign to the poet. But after the description of the unprepossessing congregation in a Zion chapel meeting on the Christmas Eve of 'Forty-nine,' its emotional tempo abruptly rises. The narrator rushes out into the evening, having had enough of 'the hot smell and the human noises,' and is confronted by the beauties of the night sky.

Alliance of Poets

> There was a lull in the rain, a lull
>   In the wind too; the moon was risen,
> And would have shone out pure and full,
>   But for the ramparted cloud-prison,
> Block on block built up in the West,
> For what purpose the wind knows best,
> Who changes his mind continually.
> And the empty other half of the sky
> Seemed in its silence as if it knew
> What, any moment, might look through
> A chance gap . . .

The imagery is suddenly clear, and there is a taut urgency about the lines. Here, outside, the poet—or the narrator—finds the ranting sermon less preposterous; the people inside had certainly felt something; 'the zeal was good and the aspiration;' only to the unconvinced was it unconvincing. This passage is, in fact, a premature statement of the whole poem's conclusion. But whilst he thus reasons concerning the relativity of religious belief,

>   . . . suddenly
> The rain and the wind ceased, and the sky
> Received at once the full fruition
> Of the moon's consummate apparition.
> The black cloud-barricade was riven,
> Ruined beneath her feet, and driven
> Deep in the West; while, bare and breathless,
>   North and South and East lay ready
> For a glorious thing that, dauntless, deathless,
>   Sprang across them and stood steady.
> 'Twas a moon-rainbow . . .

And out of the rainbow rose another rainbow, and out of the second

>   the sight
> Of a sweepy garment, vast and white,
> With a hem that I could recognize . . .

At that point the vision ceases to be convincing. For whereas the picture of the night sky suggests one of those states of heightened consciousness such as Wordsworth knew in the presence of nature, something akin too to those experiences which Tennyson called his 'weird seizures,' about the 'sweepy garment, vast and white' there clings no such aura of authenticity. The common outside the meeting house and the cloud-barred sky are lit with the harsh beam of expectancy that belongs to such moments. Clearly Browning was recalling some feeling of imminent revelation he had himself known, perhaps in his childhood. But the culmination is false; the Redeemer 'with his human air' is a lay figure, and with his introduction 'Christmas Eve' drops back to its dull discursive level.

The second of the poems, 'Easter Day', is in intention a dispute concerning the way in which man may

> at last awake
> From life, that insane dream we take
> For waking now.

But no such fundamental inquiry into man's state is, in fact, attempted; the poem is no more than an argument in which a visionary, of no greater depth of experience than the narrator of 'Christmas Eve,' is pitted against a sceptic. Elizabeth Browning complained of the asceticism of this second part. 'Don't think that he has taken to the cilix,' she wrote however, to a friend—'indeed he has not—but it is his way to *see* things as passionately as as other people *feel* them.' Clearly her habitual understanding of her husband's mind had deserted her.

It is difficult to associate that quality with anything Browning wrote. Here indeed his thought is tortured, but it is by the strait-jacket of an alien form, not by a hair-shirt. Browning was incapable of asceticism, for his valuations were coloured at all times by his fundamental belief in earthly love. So much so that when the protagonist of 'Easter Day' is condemned for his attachment to the things of this world, he immediately wakes to discover that his vision of the Judgment has been no more than a dream. Not for a moment could Browning reject the colour and richness and human variety of the temporal scene.

But this dream passage has the same intensity as the scene outside the chapel in 'Christmas Eve.' Indeed Browning, without a hint to his reader that it is finally to prove a dream and no more, sets it upon the same common that his narrator had crossed in the first poem. The coincidence plays no part in the development of 'Easter Day,' though it serves to accentuate the identification of this dreamer with the explorer of many creeds of 'Christmas Eve.' We see him first walking there, brooding only half seriously upon life and the Judgment, when suddenly he is confronted with a vision like that of 'Christmas Eve,' but even more intense. 'I found,' he says,

> Suddenly all the midnight round
> One fire. The dome of heaven had stood
> As made up of a multitude
> Of handbreadth cloudlets, one vast rack
> Of ripples infinite and black,
> From sky to sky. Sudden there went,
> Like horror and astonishment,
> A fierce vindictive scribble of red
> Quick flame across, as if one said
> (The angry scribe of Judgment) 'There—
> Burn it!'

The fierce glory in the night sky was the signal that

Doomsday had come, and the poet—or his narrator—read in it his own condemnation, for he had chosen the world, preferring in his life the finite to the infinite. Yet how, he pleads, could he have rejected it, for

> it was hard so soon
> As in a short life, to give up
> Such beauty.

So, not utterly condemned, he was sentenced to remain in that state of duality which Browning had symbolically defined in 'The Flight of the Duchess.' For while he received the gift of all the world he had so desired, he must enjoy it in the knowledge that its partial beauty was no more than a pledge of beauty in its plenitude. 'But since the pledge sufficed thy mood,' runs his sentence,

> Retain it! plenitude be theirs
> Who looked above.

So Browning might have felt when he knew himself cast down from the Shelleyan empyrean for his failure to carry through his Romantic rebellion.

Once in his youth he had known a moment of mingled terror and revelation, from which he had emerged, in *Pauline*, condemned yet treasuring that seed of hope which had grown to flower in the personal affirmation of 'Saul.' 'Christmas Eve' and 'Easter Day' together hark back to this early stage in the development of his faith. For not since his boyhood had he thought in terms of a religious choice between free-thought and the chapel. Such strengths as they have, therefore, they share rather with *Pauline* than with his mature poetry. From the reviewers they had a mixed reception. The critic of the *Athenaeum*, indeed, described their verse as doggerel, and summed up their theology perfunctorily but not unjustly in a manner that offended their author. Not till his more deeply considered poem *La Saisiaz*, twenty-eight years later, did Browning attempt again to speak in the first person of ultimate problems.

The twin poems' setting was English; in it was no trace of Italy's influence upon him. Nor did they bear any marks of the happiness he found in his marriage. Perhaps it was the death of his mother that had called his thoughts back to England. 'No day has passed since our marriage,' wrote Elizabeth to her sister-in-law, 'that he has not fondly talked of her. I know how deep in his dear heart her memory lies.' These were no facile words of condolence; the poet felt his loss very deeply. A week or two later his wife was writing that she wished she could get him to 'go somewhere or do something.' His spirits, and to some extent his health had given way. He could not think of returning to Hatcham without extreme pain. It would break his heart, he wrote, to see his mother's roses over the wall, and the place where she used to lay her scissors and gloves. Perhaps he felt no more than any man would feel; but perhaps his mother's death had the profounder effect of sending him back from the Italian present to brood on the old preoccupations of his adolescence; perhaps it contributed to the failure of his long contemplated 'poem for the times.'

On March 9th 1849, a month before Sarah Ann Browning died, Elizabeth, who was now forty-three and had suffered three miscarriages, bore him a son. That summer the Brownings left Florence on a sightseeing journey along the coast, by the pinewoods and the Carrara mountains, to the Bay of Spezzia, and settled for a while at the fashionable summer resort at the Baths of Lucca. Here they rented a house, Browning recovered his spirits, the miraculous baby throve and Elizabeth Browning was more active than ever since her girlhood. Once they rode out for a whole long day into the volcanic region of Prato Fiorito, a desolate tract scored with ravines that may have suggested the final landscape of 'Childe Roland.' It was at Lucca that Elizabeth Browning gave her husband the manuscript of those *Sonnets from the Portuguese* which she had written during their courtship and engagement. At Lucca too they met new friends: Charles Lever; the Countess Ossoli, an American woman-writer of pronounced socialist views, whose death in a shipwreck a few months later deeply shocked them both; and Miss Isa Blagden, 'a bright, delicate electric woman,' who was to be a lifelong friend. It was not till after their return to Florence that 'Christmas Eve' and 'Easter Day' were actually written. Outwardly they did not connect in any way with the circumstances of his life. For just at that time his liberal enthusiasms were at their height, so much so that he could hardly tolerate the Countess Ossoli's equally violent socialism, and expressed nothing but antipathy for her heroine George Sand. Moreover he actually refused for some time to make the acquaintance of the tory Mrs. Trollope on the grounds that she had attacked liberalism and the poetry of Victor Hugo. Who would have supposed that inwardly he was taken up with theological broodings?

In the later summer of 1850 Elizabeth Browning fell ill, and in September they moved to Siena, she in a miserably helpless state, as she told her sister, having to be lifted about like a baby, looking ghostly rather than ghastly. The cause appears to have been yet another miscarriage, which she had suffered in July. But soon she had recovered, and they were back in Florence. In the spring of the next year they were once more travel-

Alliance of Poets 71

ling, first to Venice, for a fortnight which would have been prolonged had not the place affected Browning's sleep and appetite, then to Padua, Brescia, Milan, across the Gotthard, through Switzerland to Strasburg. They had been uncertain at first whether they would make for London. Certainly they would not be going for the sake of the Exposition, Elizabeth assured Miss Mitford. 'If by any arrangement I could see my sister Arabel in France or on the coast of England, we would persuade Robert's family to meet us there, and not see London at all. Ah, if you knew how abhorrent the thought of England is to *me*! . . . My eyes shut suddenly when my thoughts go that way.' In London was Mr. Barrett, still inflexible, perhaps more inflexible indeed since recently a second daughter had escaped him. In Paris by chance they met the Tennysons, who hearing that they had nowhere to go in England, offered them Chapel House for as long as they liked, with the servants and all that it contained. Robert Browning was deeply touched, but it was not to Twickenham that they went. They took lodgings in Devonshire Street within a few hundred yards of the Wimpole Street house from which Elizabeth Browning had eloped. Their friendship with Tennyson, however, grew stronger. Only the year before Elizabeth Browning had been passed over in his favour, when at Wordsworth's death a successor had been chosen for the Laureateship. Her claims had been quite strenuously advanced; none had been put forth on behalf of her husband. But now all three were united in mutual esteem.

Back in London after five years, the Brownings were welcomed by his old literary friends. Forster gave a dinner in their honour; Rogers invited them both to breakfast; they spent an evening with Carlyle. Arnould too, the friend of Browning's youth, proposed that they should share his house, and Miss Haworth, his confidante in the days of his theatrical ambitions, quickly won the friendship of Elizabeth to whom she lent some books on mesmerism and Swedenborg, subjects that were later to obtain considerable hold on the poetess's imagination. For the first time too she met her husband's father and sister; her own sisters were constant visitors. But her father's door remained resolutely shut. He returned her in a packet all the letters she had written to him, unopened. Depression at this, perhaps, and the effect of England upon her health sent the Brownings back to Paris after a couple of months. He, as the visit proved, had retained and perhaps increased his large circle of literary acquaintances; as a poet, however, he stood no higher in public regard than when he had left the country in 1846.

Chapter Four

SONG'S OUR ART

> 'Tis you speak, that's your error. Song's our art:
> Whereas you please to speak these naked thoughts
> Instead of draping them in sights and sounds.

IN these three lines from the poem 'Transcendentalism.' Browning proclaimed his abandonment of the false way up which he had been endeavouring to force a passage in *Christmas Eve and Easter Day*. Henceforth he would give up the poetry of argument for the poetry of magic, forsake speech for incantation. To that extreme he did not in fact go; his future poetry was to be poetry of argument, but not poetry spoken in the first person. Sometimes only would it be song, but always, at its best, it would sing more clearly and more tunefully than the halting verse of those two poems.

'Transcendentalism' is a curious piece, that shows, for once, the limitations of Browning's reading and understanding. For out of all the possible figures he could have selected to represent the speaking of naked thoughts he could not have found one more suitable than the mystical writer Jakob Boehme. Boehme, according to some anecdote which the poet had no doubt discovered in his father's library long ago, was remarkable for his completely negative attitude to the world's beauty, paying no attention to nature. In fact, Browning tells us, he

> never cared for plants
> Until it happed, a-walking in the fields,
> He noticed all at once that plants could speak . . .

In contrast to Boehme, the representative of this intellectual approach, Browning drew the picture of one John of Halberstadt, a nature mystic, whom he described a as 'magician, botanist and a chymist,' who

> With a 'Look you!' vents a brace of rhymes,
> And in there breaks the sudden rose herself,
> Over us, under, round us every side,
> Nay, in and out the tables and the chairs
> And musty volumes, Boehme's book and all,—
> Buries us with a glory, young once more,
> Pouring heaven into this shut house of life.

The moral is sound enough, though the illustration is strange. But this poem, the first of the *Men and Women*, is important in a further sense. For it is charged with just that symbolism which had been so painfully excluded from its twin predecessor. The rose, in this connection, has the same magic significance for Browning as later it was to have for Yeats. It is the symbol of eternal life, of the renewal of youth and of the triune experience of Love—Creation—Faith that is the burden of 'Saul.' In 'Transcendentalism' the flower is associated with the act of poetic creation; in 'Women and Roses,' a poem far less precise in its allegory, it is linked to the idea of love, and in 'The Heretic's Tragedy' the rose of fire is used in a negative sense, as the symbol of a false consuming faith. for the heretical Templar burns at the stake. In imagery rich in that sense of the horrible of which he was at times a master, Browning describes how

> . . . petal on petal, fierce rays unclose;
> Anther on anther, sharp spikes outstart;
> And with blood for dew, the bosom boils;

'Women and Roses,' though important for its use of the rose symbol and for the statement it just fails to make, is at best an unsatisfactory poem. Mrs. Sutherland Orr speaks of it as the impression of a dream, and both vague and vivid, as such impressions are. The poet dreams of a red rose tree with three roses upon it, one withered, the second full blown and the third still in bud. To him they represent the generations of women dead, living and unborn. Each he endeavours in turn to worship, and each eludes him, for all three 'circle their rose on my rose tree': the phrase is ambiguous. The poet, however, seems to picture himself as in the centre, with the processions of maidens dancing round him, but himself unable to touch them since they are always in motion. The quest for the rose, whether successful or unsuccessful, whether it elude the dreamer of 'Women and Roses' or rise to the spell of John of Halberstadt, symbolizes in fresh form Robert Browning's most urgent preoccupation. For the note of intellectual conviction with which 'Easter Day' closes, the sonorous affirmation of 'Saul' and the Duchess's escape into the gipsy country are none of them earnests of final achievement; in his poetry the quest must be perpetually renewed, possession of the rose is never assured. Browning's was essentially a miraculous view of the world. For he had always the suspicion that life held surprising and magical possibilities for the man who should guess its secret. In three other poems which, like those just cited, appeared in his *Men and Women*, he gives conflicting pictures of what this secret might be. First one finds it in 'The Guardian Angel' described in terms of a healing or, more precisely, of relief from the tortures of an over-active brain. But here he is able to picture this different state of being only imprecisely in terms once more of the triune beauty-love-duty:

> How soon all worldly wrong would be repaired!
> I think how I should view the earth and skies
> And sea, when once again my brow was bared
> After thy healing, with such different eyes.
> O world, as God has made it! All is beauty:
> And knowing this, is love, and love is duty.
> What further may be sought for or declared?

But, in one of the loveliest poems in *Men and Women*—'Love among the Ruins'—one finds it conceived of less intellectually, in terms of pure peace and love in a land that has grown quiet after the passing of empires. A much more profound statement, however, of that other life occurs in 'An Epistle containing the Strange Medical Experience of Karshish the Arab Physician', a poem in which an incredulous traveller describes a meeting with the raised Lazarus—'a Jew, sanguine, proportioned, fifty years of age,'—and reflects upon the claims of 'the Nazarene who wrought this cure' to be . . .

> God forgive me! who but God himself,
> Creator and sustainer of the world,
> That came and dwelt in flesh on it awhile!

This 'Epistle,' 'Cleon' and 'A Death in the Desert,' all three among Browning's very finest achievements, are attempts to present the miraculous story of Christ with varying degrees of obliquity, the first two as seen through the eyes of inquiring pagans, and the third as reflected in the memory of the dying St. John, the last witness and the first to foresee the age of mingled hope and doubt that would come after him. But whereas St. John is waking for the last time, and speaks with the other-worldly assurance of one who has almost died, Lazarus has indeed gone down into the grave and returned. Now he is no longer attached to the things of the world, but is waiting patiently to be released into that other country where he can employ the treasure he gained in his short sojourn there. 'We call the treasure knowledge,' explains the Arab Physician, 'knowledge

> Increased beyond the fleshly faculty—
> Heaven opened to a soul while yet on earth,
> Earth forced on a soul's use while seeing heaven:
> The man is witless of the size, the sum,
> The value in proportion of all things,
> Or whether it be little or be much . . .
> The man is apathetic, you deduce?
> Contrariwise, he loves both old and young,
> Able and weak, affects the very brutes
> And birds—how say I? flowers of the field—
> As a wise workman recognizes tools
> In a master's workshop, loving what they make.

Whether his grail be symbolized as a treasure, a rose, or the completed triad of faith, love and creation, or beauty, love and duty, Browning's finest poems are a varied record of the quest for it.

The most important and symbolically the richest of these quest poems is 'Childe Roland to the Dark Tower came,' a piece generally classed with 'The Flight of the Duchess' as pure romance. Mrs. Sutherland Orr in her *Handbook*, however, labels it a moralizing allegory, in contrast to 'The Flight' which she calls a moralizing fairy tale. 'They are both,' she adds, 'a useful type both of Mr. Browning's poetic genius, and of the misunderstanding to which its constantly intellectual employment has exposed him.' The poet of 'Christmas Eve,' in other words, was expected to make plain statements; his public has forgotten the obscurities of *Sordello* and knew nothing of the emotional complexities of *Pauline*. Mrs. Orr, however, knew the nature of his genius better. She was besides in his confidence.

'Childe Roland' was written in Paris in a single day, January 3rd 1852. 'Love among the Ruins' and 'Women and Roses' had been written on the 1st and 2nd respectively. These are among the few poems of Browning's that can be exactly dated.

The first suggestion for 'Childe Roland' came from a line of Edgar's in *Lear*: 'Child Rowland to the dark tower came,' a line as suggestive as that snatch of a song which had given Browning his inspiration for 'The Flight of the Duchess.' Both poems reach down to the emotional levels at which dualities and congruities are as one. For as the huntsman and the Duke in the earlier poem were but two aspects of the same figure, so the cripple of 'Childe Roland's' opening lines is both a false and a true guide.

> What else should he be set for, with his staff?
>   What, save to waylay with his lies, ensnare
>   All travellers who might find him posted there,
> And ask the road? I guessed what skull-like laugh
> Would break, what crutch 'gin write my epitaph
>   For pastime in the dusty thoroughfare,
>
> If at his counsel I should turn aside
>   Into that ominous tract which, all agree,
>   Hides the Dark Tower. Yet acquiescingly
> I did turn as he pointed: neither pride
> Nor hope rekindling at the end descried,
>   So much as gladness that some end might be.

But what was the cripple's lie? For he was not standing there to waylay travellers, certain of their destination, to some treacherous death in the waste. His lie, if lie it was, was only his means of luring them from a false goal to a true one. For Childe Roland's 'worldwide wandering,' his 'search drawn out thro' years' had been in fact a search for that very secret to be won in the ordeal at the Dark Tower. The lie was not on the cripple's tongue but in Roland's own heart, and it was not so much a lie as a betrayal of his purpose, a desire to avoid that 'ominous tract' and the secret it held. There is obvious relevance in this situation to Browning's former half-hearted rebellion, seen by him still in these same terms of betrayal; his 'lying' wish was for a failure which would excuse him from further endeavours, for a collapse like that of the poet of *Pauline*.

Once the knight had turned despairingly away from 'that hateful cripple,' into the path up which he pointed, resolved deliberately to incur that failure which would bring an end to his search, all possibility of return disappeared.

> For mark! no sooner was I fairly found
>   Pledged to the plain, after a pace or two,
>   Than, pausing to throw backward a last view
> O'er the safe road, 'twas gone; grey plain all round:
> Nothing but plain to the horizon's bound.
>   I might go on; nought else remained to do.

He was now riding through a desolate country, symbolizing some lesser 'dark night of the soul,' where Nature herself was starved and ignoble, through a country of weeds and stones that could only be purged by utter burning. For, in Nature's own words to the knight as he rides through it;

> 'Tis the Last Judgment's fire must cure this place,
>   Calcine its clods and set my prisoners free.

The poet of 'Easter Day' had denied the reality of the Judgment, had woken to find it all a dream, yet with a certainty gained in that dream could confute the sceptic with whom he argued. The poet of 'Childe Roland,' however, drawing on far deeper levels of experience, describes the cruelty and ugliness of this country, through which his Everyman must conduct his search, with haunting exactness. Browning's frequent return to themes of brutality and melodramatic disgust, his startling use of images repulsive in their physical horror, arose from his deep, though only sporadic, realization that the soul of unregenerate man presents an extremely ugly picture. His optimism, for which he was so often reproached, lay in his belief that a treasure existed and could be found, by which a man could be saved. Nowhere, indeed, is his imagery so hideously obsessed as in the description of that country through which the knight, only half willingly, rode to find that ray of hope which is not permitted to break in until the poem's last verse. But here, in all its desolation, is the 'waste land' that awaits the Judgment's fire:

> As for the grass, it grew as scant as hair
>   In leprosy: thin dry blades pricked the mud
>   Which underneath looked kneaded up with blood.
> One stiff blind horse, his every bone a-stare,
> Stood stupefied, however he came there:
>   Thrust out past service from the devil's stud!
>
> Alive? he might be dead for aught I know,
>   With that red gaunt and colloped neck a-strain,
>   And shut eyes underneath the rusty mane;
> Seldom went such grotesqueness with such woe;
> I never saw a beast I hated so;
>   He must be wicked to deserve such pain.

Roland tries to summon courage by recalling the happiness of his youth, and the faces of his brothers or comrades of that time. It was, Browning knew, only with the strength of his own happy childhood that he

Song's our Art

had been able to stand up to the Shelleyan temptation of later days; the stages of the 'Childe Roland' allegory are matched exactly to those of his own history. But each of these comrades—or of his former selves—had fallen into disgrace. Just as there was no return once he had followed the cripple's path, so there was no strength to be gained by returning in spirit to a former state, which to closer view betrayed earlier instances of failure. There was nothing for it but to ride on without hope.

> Better this present than a past like that;
>   Back therefore to my darkening path again!
>   No sound, no sight as far as eye could strain.
> Will the night send a howlet or a bat?
> I asked: when something on the dismal flat
>   Came to arrest my thoughts and change their train.
>
> A sudden little river crossed my path
>   As unexpected as a serpent comes.
>   No sluggish tide congenial to the glooms;
> This, as it frothed by, might have been a bath
> For the fiend's glowing hoof—to see the wrath
>   Of its black eddy bespate with flakes and spumes.

So by fording this murky swift-flowing Styx, fearful every moment of setting a foot on a dead man's cheek, or thrusting a supporting spear in his tangled hair, the knight pushes on into what he vainly hopes may prove a better country, although trodden down by the feet of stragglers who had passed through it before him to face the fight in that 'fell cirque.' Into this arena, in which each in turn must confront his unnamed opponent, lead many footsteps, but out of it come none. 'What penned them there,' asks the knight, 'with all the plain to choose?' Why with apparent free will must each man go compulsively to the same hopeless ordeal in this deathlike country? But his question finds its own answer. When he arrives, Roland acknowledges a baleful foreknowledge of the place; there were no other tracks over the plain that he was free to follow.

> Yet half I seemed to recognize some trick
>   Of mischief happened to me, God knows when—
>   In a bad dream perhaps. Here ended, then,
> Progress this way. When, in the very nick
> Of giving up, one time more, came a click
>   As when a trap shuts—you're inside the den!
>
> Burningly it came on me all at once,
>   This was the place! those two hills on the right,
>   Crouched like two bulls locked horn in horn in fight;
> While to the left, a tall scalped mountain . . . Dunce,
> Dotard, a-dozing at the very nonce,
>   After a life spent training for the sight!

Suddenly Childe Roland recognizes the inevitability of his quest, and knows that he has spent his whole life preparing for the ordeal confronting him, an ordeal in which each of the knights before him, his brothers or his former selves, Cuthbert and Giles, and the rest, has been vanquished. Yet have they been vanquished? For, in the poem's final stanza,

> There they stood, ranged along the hill-sides, met
>   To view the last of me, a living frame
>   For one more picture! in a sheet of flame
> I saw them and I knew them all. And yet
> Dauntless the slug-horn to my lips I set
>   And blew. '*Childe Roland to the Dark Tower came.*'

The poem remains half-resolved; its ambiguities are not dispelled. There is no dream-like escape into any land of the gipsies; not so much as a glimpse of a promised country into which that dauntless horn-blast may purchase admission. The poem's landscape reveals no hint of beauty even at the last; it is throughout one with the Duke's other country of 'The Flight,' one vast red drear burnt-up plain; but it presents another and far more unexpected parallel. It is into that same land that the Arab physician rode to learn of Lazarus' raising and to hear news of the 'Nazarene physician.'

> I have shed sweat enough, left flesh and bone
> On many a flinty furlong of this land,

says Karshish in the introduction, and at the poem's conclusion he expands his description of the place in which he came upon the sanguine, well-proportioned, fifty-year-old revenant from beyond the grave. 'I met him thus,' he writes:

> I crossed a ridge of short sharp broken hills
> Like an old lion's cheek teeth. Out there came
> A moon made like a face with certain spots
> Multiform, manifold and menacing . . .

The imagery is far less brutal than that of 'Childe Roland' and preserves the microscopic exactness attributed to the scientific Karshish. But the landscape is the same; and it is remarkable, also, that the setting of that other and later poem concerned with the Gospel revelation, 'A Death in the Desert,' is set in country of the same unrelieved desolation, country in which a single goat has nothing to graze on but

> rags of various herb,
> Plantain and quitch, the rocks' shade keeps alive.

The scenery of mountains seems inevitable. For though the quest in 'Childe Roland' began over a plain, at the end and unexpectedly the knight found

> the plain had given place
> All round to mountains—with such name to grace
> Mere ugly heights and heaps now stolen in view.

The purpose of the quest might seem to be, therefore, the witnessing of some miracle among the mountains, yet ultimately the miracle, if miracle there was, was unwitnessed, and the poet remained in his 'waste land.' Only on the plans of escape or fantasy could the other way of living be imagined; in reality it was not the Judgment but any hope of avoiding or by-passing it that was a dream.

Associated with 'Childe Roland' by the nearby dates of their composition are the mysterious 'Women and Roses' —which seems to recall some failure of a parallel quest— and the smooth and half sleepy 'Love among the Ruins,' whose assured, softly chiming rhythms suggest repletion and rest. But the setting of this last poem, the first of the three in order of composition, as 'Childe Roland' is the last, is a landscape rich with memorials of other and earlier defeats.

> Now,—the single little turret that remains
>   On the plains,
> By the caper overrooted, by the gourd
>   Overscored,
> While the patching houseleek's head of blossom winks
>   Through the chinks—
> Marks the basement whence a tower in ancient time
>   Sprang sublime,
> And a burning ring, all round, the chariots traced
>   As they raced,
> And the monarch and his minions and his dames
>   Viewed the games.

Was it to some such land that Roland was riding when

Song's our Art

the lying cripple lured him into the waste? This poem has no ambiguities. On the gravestones of an earlier civilization, among the memorials of efforts that have failed, it is possible for Browning, with a ring of certainty that is corroborated by the certain beat of each rhyme, to consign the glories and triumphs of the past to the dust and, in the certainty that 'a girl with eager eyes and yellow hair' will keep her tryst among the ruins, proclaim in his final line that 'Love is best.'

Browning's visits to his 'waste land' were few. The 'Flight of the Duchess' records an escape from it on the plane of fantasy into a country that he wished to describe but could not; 'Christmas Eve' and 'Easter Day' state a false solution of the dilemma he found there; and 'Childe Roland' tells of a journey through its desolation to face an ordeal of which he could picture neither the nature nor the outcome.

In a poem that sprang from far less profound levels of experience than were tapped by the intrusive associations of 'Following the Queen of the Gypsies, O!' or of the fragmentary line from *Lear*, Browning reverted once more to his dilemma, analysing it this time in terms of musical composition; the piece concerns an imaginary composer, Master Hugues of Saxe Gotha. Here the contrast is between the complication of a fugue made up of so many contradictory voices and the full organ blaring out 'the mode Palestrina.' Is all this 'affirming, denying, holding, risposting, subjoining,' the unknown organist asks the ghost of the musician, what he supposes life to be.

> Is it your moral of Life?
>   Such a web, simple and subtle,
> Weave we on earth here in impotent strife,
>   Backward and forward each throwing his shuttle,
> Death ending all with a knife?

It is through our zig-zags and dodges, he complains, that God's gold is covered beneath the pall of man's usurpature—and experience overlaid by intellectualization.

> So we o'ershroud stars and roses,
>   Cherub and trophy and garland;
> Nothings grow something which quietly closes
>   Heaven's earnest eye: not a glimpse of the far land
> Gets through our comments and glozes.

Far from rejoicing in his philosophical and intellectual complexity—as the Browning society supposed—Robert Browning here, half humorously perhaps, but nevertheless with genuine conviction, wrote the complexities off as mere obscuring cobwebs and comforted himself with the assurance that, nevertheless,

> Truth's golden o'er us although we refuse it.

But 'Master Hugues of Saxe Gotha' is too lightweight a poem to be tortured into yielding so deep a moral; its 'stars and roses' are only by remote inference to be identified with the objects of Browning's quest.

For the symbolism of the quest and the waste land, though profoundly important to Browning, nevertheless plays a part in only a few of his poems. These mark the activity of the poet of *Pauline* continued into middle life, but preoccupied now not with the resolution of adolescent half-rebellion, but with the search for life's secret purpose, a treasure by contrast to which commonplace objects and events seem sordid and brutal. Many more of his poems, however, are concerned with human love, an experience which raises the everyday world to beauty, and shuts out all sight of that desolate plain which leads to the distant mountains. It appears, one might say, to offer at least a provisional solution for problems, which, in their ultimate and metaphysical sense, are insoluble except in terms of an intuitive and elusive hope.

'By the Fireside,' perhaps the most personal of Browning's love poems, containing as it does the portrait of Elizabeth,

> Reading by fire-light, that great brow
> And the spirit-small hand propping it . . .

looks back from an imaginary middle age on a wooing transposed to Italy, and set in a mountain landscape milder than that of the Duke's other country, yet vaguely recalling it. The actual scene against which Browning reconstructed his wooing of Elizabeth was copied from a valley near Florence where they had walked together a year or two before. The detail is faithfully recorded in all its intimate desolation:

> Look at the ruined chapel again,
>   Half-way up in the Alpine gorge!
> Is that a tower, I point you plain,
>   Or is it a mill, or an iron-forge
> Breaks solitude in vain?

Like 'The Flight of the Duchess,' this poem is concerned with two contrasted climates. But here they are not geographical alternatives. Here they are thought of as man and woman: 'woman's country' and 'earth's male lands.' What in the earlier poem might appear to be two aspects of a single mind, the poet's, was here embodied in two people; and the union or reconciliation required not a flight or escape, but their union, after Shelley's platonic fashion, to form one soul and pass beyond life as one. In 'By the Fireside' Browning glimpsed for a moment, perhaps, that other, magic country which he had not been able to describe before, in which the Queen lived at peace with her gipsy lover. Yet he could only hint at its nature by adapting a biblical phrase for his culminating line.

> Think, when our one soul understands
>   The great Word which makes all things new,
> When earth breaks up and heaven expands,
>   How will the change strike me and you
> In the house not made with hands?

But though that is the poem's central question, 'By the Fireside' has few verses so abstract and ethereal. It is in the main a celebration of the beauties of the world and of human love, rich in observed and affectionate detail and failing only in one place, in its apostrophe to 'My perfect wife, my Leonor,' a line which partakes of the same sentimental falsity as that of 'sweepy garment, vast and white, with a hem that I could recognize,' of 'Christmas Eve.' For when Browning attempted to convey the highest emotion, the deepest experience, each time he failed. If he had experienced them it was too fleetingly, with too excited a vision, to allow of his recording them. So he was reduced to describing the heights of love or revelation in other men's words, and sometimes with fatal banality. But in his choice of the biblical 'house not made with hands,' and even more magically in describing the Christ of 'A Death in the Desert,' in words borrowed from the Apocalypse of St. John:

With head wool-white, eyes flame, and feet like brass,
The sword and the seven stars, as I have seen . . .

Browning heightened the emotion of his poem, passing from his own words to those of the Bible without the least break; a feat which might not have been possible

Song's our Art

but for the biblical strand which was a more or less constant constituent of his more serious style.

'By the Fireside' is the most important of the love poems in *Men and Women*, but there are others devoted to pursuit and wooing, winning and loss, in which the same lyrical note prevails, pieces such as 'A Lovers' Quarrel,' 'The Last Ride Together,' 'Love in a Life,' 'Life in a Love,' concerned with more imaginary situations, snatches often of pure rapture, though not without occasional drops into bathos and sentimentality. For although Browning was not a poet of the highest lyrical attainments except in short flights, and was conscious of the fact, he held that love poetry should be written on a sustained lyrical note, and was willing to strain his voice in order to maintain it. So in effect he states in the dedicatory 'One Word More' with which he presents his book to 'E.B.B.' Every artist, he says, would wish to give to his beloved a work for her eyes alone, performed in a medium that was not his own. Raphael made a century of sonnets for his lady, Dante painted a picture of Beatrice, but he, Robert Browning, will never

> Paint you pictures, no, nor carve you statues,
> Make you music that should all-express me. . .

In this dedication, however, he will give her something more intimate, for her eyes alone.

> Love, you saw me gather men and women,
> Live or dead or fashioned by my fancy,
> Enter each and all, and use their service,
> Speak from every mouth,—the speech, a poem.

This, as Browning saw it, was what he had done in creating his 'Karshish, Cleon, Norbert and the fifty.'

They were no part of him, but objective portraits or creations that he could hand over to the public, in the confidence that they would not tell of his joys and his sorrows. But in 'One Word More' he resolved to speak for once in his true person, 'not as Lippo, Roland or Andrea.' A strangely various trio these, for none of his characters betrayed more of Browning's inner experience than Roland, and few came nearer to the status of objective personages existing in their own right than his two painters Fra Lippo Lippi and Andrea del Sarto.

The two blank verse monologues bearing their names stand in the third group of Browning's *Men and Women*, being concerned with the third of his triune qualities, the act of creation, and with questions of character and philosophic beliefs. They are—to use the distinction made in 'Master Hugues of Saxe Gotha'—fugues, to be contrasted with the unstopping of the full organ in 'By the Fireside,' in 'One Word More' and—little though Browning would have acknowledged the fact—in 'Childe Roland.' 'Andrea del Sarto,' 'Fra Lippo Lippi' and 'Cleon' are three variations on the single theme of art's inadequacy as a way of life. The conclusion is overtly stated in 'Cleon' and merely implied in the two Italian pieces. For del Sarto, both as lover and artist, has fallen short of his ideal; lacking any glimpse of the third pole of faith, he has failed to exploit his perfect painter's technique and is content to be deceived by a wife whom he still feebly loves. The poem is as sad in tone as 'Fra Lippo Lippi' is lively. For poor brother Lippi is a creature of a fine earthy humour, with somewhere beneath his monkish cloak the innocent heart of a Pippa. He is the true artist, content to catch whatever he can of the soul by painting the body, to enjoy his 'lights of love,' and catch

Song's our Art

the likenesses of his patrons and superiors without thought for the morrow or the hereafter. Yet there are moments when he too is filled with some other intuition, that he does not pause to analyse, when

> . . . some warm eve finds me at my saints—
> A laugh, a cry, the business of the world—
> (*Flower o' the peach,*
> *Death for us all, and his own life for each!*)
> And my whole soul revolves, the cup runs over,
> The world and life's too big to pass for a dream,
> And I do these wild things in sheer despite,
> And play the fooleries you catch me at,
> In pure rage!

Such is Lippo Lippi, simple and unregenerate, artist but no lover, sly, vigorous, humorous and intoxicated with the vanity of the world, a monk without a vocation, a painter with a true eye for the prettiest face and a naïve certainty that

> If you get simple beauty and nought else,
> You get about the best thing God invents.

But if the monkish painter is content to be a pagan, the pagan Cleon is unsatisfied with the immortality he can gain through art; his old age is no more tolerable to him for his paintings, his carvings or the odes he has made. For what is it, he asks, that will survive him?

> The brazen statue to o'erlook my grave,
> Set on the promontory which I named.
> And that—some supple courtier of my heir
> Shall use its robed and sceptred arm, perhaps,
> To fix the rope to, which best drags it down.

Body and soul will alike perish in death. The prospect is so horrible that he can at times imagine

> Some future state revealed to us by Zeus,
> Unlimited in capability
> For joy, as this is in desire for joy. . .

But as for the promise of some such state made by the barbarian Jew Paulus, and lately preached upon Cleon's own isle by certain slaves, he cannot trouble himself even to investigate the story, for

> Their doctrine could be held by no sane man.

Bishop Blougram, who holds that doctrine, though with reservations that he does not clearly define, is a very sane man, the sanest perhaps of all the *Men and Women*. He may contain something of Father Prout and, as Browning himself admitted, be intended in part as a portrait of Cardinal Wiseman, the first Roman Catholic Archbishop of Westminster, but he speaks in part also for his creator. For 'Bishop Blougram's Apology' continues the argument of *Christmas Eve and Easter Day*, though now the speaker is far less closely associated with the poet himself than were the two hardly contrasted protagonists of faith in those earlier poems. Browning had, as has been seen, no profound understanding of Catholicism. He saw it, nevertheless, as a creed capable of dealing with the problems of the world in worldly terms. Divorced of its grosser superstitions, to which, the poem suggests, its educated leaders do not subscribe, it represented for him a position to be defended against the theorists of the German lecture halls, and the paying materialism of Blougram's shadowy interlocutor, Gigadibs. Blougram's was at least a teaching 'not so obscured that no truth shines athwart the lies,' but one on a lower level than a man might reach, riding out by the light of his own spark. 'The common problem,' Blougram says,

Song's our Art

> Is—not to fancy what were fair in life
> Provided it could be,—but, finding first
> What may be, then find how to make it fair
> Up to our means . . .

This is a more cautious and tentative position than Browning's own. But the Bishop, nevertheless, speaks for his creator in so far as he refers all problems back ultimately to faith. 'See the world such as it is,' he says, 'you made it not nor I. I mean to take it as it is.' And as it is, he finds that faith is the principal element in it. Napoleon could not with comfort to himself have blown millions up but for 'his crazy trust God knows through what or in what.' So, faith being a necessary constituent of life, let it be a reasonable faith. Perhaps Blougram is understating his case. For, says Browning at the end, he believed, say, half he spoke.

The rest was the sprightliest of verbal conjuring intended to discomfort his journalistic visitor. Perhaps Browning means us to assume that the Bishop tempered the statement of his belief in order to meet Mr. Gigadibs on his own ground. Yet at the moment when he defines his attitude to faith the temperature of the poem rises appreciably from its steady argumentative level, the dialectic swelling to dramatic statement, a certain sign that the poet was here speaking for himself as well as for his character. The moment is one in which the Bishop dismisses an imaginary objection of his interviewer's, with an argument foreshadowing the dying St. John's in 'A Death in the Desert.'

> Pure faith indeed—you know not what you ask!
> Naked belief in God the Omnipotent,
> Omniscient, Omnipresent, sears too much
> The sense of conscious creatures to be borne.
> It were the seeing him, no flesh shall dare.

> Some think, Creation's meant to show him forth:
> I say it's meant to hide him all it can,
> And that's what all the blessed evil's for.
> Its use in Time is to environ us,
> Our breath, our drop of dew, with shield enough
> Against that sight till we can bear its stress.
> Under a vertical sun, the exposed brain
> And lidless eye and disemprisoned heart
> Less certainly would wither up at once
> Than mind, confronted with the truth of him.
> But time and earth case-harden us to live;
> The feeblest sense is trusted most; the child
> Feels God a moment, ichors o'er the place,
> Plays on and grows to be a man like us.
> With me, faith means perpetual unbelief
> Kept quiet like the snake 'neath Michael's foot
> Who stands calm just because he feels it writhe . . .
> Say I—let doubt occasion still more faith!

This is Browning's own statement of his everyday fight for conviction; of the mood in which with Roland he approached the Dark Tower, set the slug-horn to his lips, but had no sight of whatever grail he was seeking; of the mood in which the hunter accompanied his Duchess to the borders of the gipsy country, but brought back no news of the life there; of the mood in which Browning himself replied to Robert Buchanan's question whether he were a Christian with a thunderous 'No.' It was not the mood of the end of 'Saul.' Browning's moments of revelation were few; the triangle of love—creation—faith was seldom completed in a single poem or a single moment of vision. For him, as for Blougram, however, evil and doubt existed only in order to occasion faith. So the temporizing Roman Catholic archbishop, like each one of Browning's men and women, spoke for one aspect of the man himself. For in his great monologues Browning rang the changes on his own constituent moods or personalities, embodying each in turn in a character who should hold the stage and, in defending, expounding and pleading his own case, speak in part also for his creator. There was Blougram, the man of intellect who made a virtue of his emotional limitations; Andrea del Sarto, the perfect artist whose creative powers were hampered by emotional shortcomings of another kind; Lippo Lippi, the pagan creator overwhelmed at moments by a melancholy that testified to some deeper experience he was missing; Cleon, another pagan, unable to content himself with the world of art, yet overlooking his one clue to the profound truth he was half in search of; and Karshish, almost distrustful of his scientific detachment when confronted with an event beyond his powers to explain. All are different, yet all share one feature in common: a conviction, an intimation or perhaps no more than an inkling that there is some truth a little beyond their comprehension, the realization of which would alter the whole of their values. It is perhaps his consciousness of just this that Blougram is most anxious to disguise from his prying interviewer. All are different, yet all speak for Browning himself, and testify to his own search for the secret which would be Childe Roland's reward for the dauntless hornblast with which he confronted the Dark Tower, the secret that David knew when in the full outpouring of love and song he attained a moment of true emotional faith.

When the two volumes of *Men and Women* appeared in 1855, the year of Tennyson's far more successful *Maud*, they received a better reception than Browning had yet met with, but still hardly an adequate one. There were the old complaints of his obscurities, though it was admitted that he had grown in power and originality to a degree which compensated for them. Elizabeth was pleased with the great deal of notice the book aroused, though she admitted that the reviews contained 'abuse as well as laudation.' Only the pre-Raphaelites greeted *Men and Women* with unmixed enthusiasm. A letter from Ruskin, indeed, loud in praise of the 'Epistle of Karshish' arrived on the same day as one from Elizabeth's sister Henrietta, revealing her secret disgust at what she took to be the poem's blasphemous implications. Elizabeth replied to her reassuringly, if a little too firmly, that 'among all the criticisms we have heard, private and public, such an idea as yours seems to have occured to no one.' Browning's purpose in writing it, she went on, had been in the highest degree reverential and Christian. It was perhaps not for those virtues that William Bell Scott acclaimed this same poem, putting it on a level with 'Blougram's Apology' and describing it in a letter to W. M. Rossetti as 'beyond all inventions he has yet done.' Browning himself was less flattered by praise from these rather dubious quarters than by the appreciation of his French friend Joseph Milsand, in an article in the *Revue Contemporaine*. For whereas most of his English critics supposed him to be aiming at the utmost objectivity, discussing his *Men and Women* as dramatic characters, created to speak with voices of their own, Milsand saw that Browning's inspiration partook of the subjective and objective alike. He considered that Browning was first an introspective poet, and only secondarily an artist or 'maker.' 'His explorations,' he had written of earlier poems, 'are adventures of the intellect; his faculties expand themselves *within*.' Now in reviewing *Men and Women* he re-stressed this opinion. 'I am inclined to think,' he wrote, 'that this constant endeavour has been to reconcile and combine his talents, so as to be not in turn but simultaneously, lyrical and dramatic, subjective and objective.' Milsand perhaps attributed to his English friend a more conscious purpose than he in fact possessed, but Browning knew how close his friend had come to understanding his true achievement.

After leaving London in 1851, the Brownings had spent part of the winter in Paris, where the first of his *Men and Women* and the introduction to some spurious Shelley letters were composed. It was here that they had first met Milsand, who was writing an article on Elizabeth Browning's poetry, and came to Browning for guidance. This Frenchman had studied art and fallen under Ruskin's influence. Then abandoning the role of painter he had set out to interpret the English critic in France. At the same time he had abandoned Catholicism and fought his way to an independent Protestantism that must have had much in common with Browning's own. After that he had begun writing articles on the English poets, starting with Tennyson and Browning. So it was that the friendship was already half made when the pair first met. It lasted for more than thirty years.

From Paris the Brownings returned to London for the summer of 1852, which they filled with the same round of social engagements as in 1851. Here they met Charles Kingsley, whom they liked despite his 'wild and theoretical' socialism; here Jane Carlyle brought Mazzini to visit them; here Rossetti, William Allingham, and Ruskin called: and here on September 5th Robert stood godfather to Alfred Tennyson's son Hallam. Then by way of Paris and the Mont Cenis they returned to Italy and their Florentine home, which they had left eighteen months before. For the next three years they remained in that country, and it was during those years that the bulk of *Men and Women* was written. Company at Florence was much scantier than in London or Paris. There were the few American expatriates, chief among them the Storys. There was Robert Lytton, the novelist's son, Frederick Tennyson, Miss Blagden, but life in Florence meant for them both an existence almost exclusively in each other's company. Here they wrote, each in a separate room, neither showing the other any work until it was completed. Here they joined one another for long and intimate evenings, united in discussion of art and politics and in their worship of their phenomenal child, nicknamed Penini, whose every infant saying was recorded for the benefit of their correspondents. 'It was delightful to find ourselves in the old nest, still warm, of Casa Guidi,' wrote Elizabeth on her return, 'to sit in our own chairs and sleep in our own beds . . . You can't think how we have caught up our ancient traditions just where we left them, and relapsed into our former soundless, stirless hermit life. Robert has not passed an evening from home since we came—just as if we had never known Paris. People come sometimes to have tea and talk with us, but that's all. . . .' It was here during the winter that Elizabeth's interest was first roused by spiritualism. But for a while experiments were confined to table-turning, and the tables generally refused to turn for the Brownings and Lytton or who ever came. Then after a summer at the Baths of Lucca, the Brownings and the Storys set off to winter in Rome. Here they met with almost as much company as in London or Paris, and soon Browning was sitting to two portrait painters at once. Here they met Thackeray, the Kemble sisters, the veteran Lockhart[1]

[1] Who took a great fancy to the poet, because he was so unlike 'a damned literary man.'

and all the Anglo-American colony settled in that city; serious work in Rome was impossible.

Back in Florence in the spring of 1854 Browning tried to make up for the time he had wasted in society by setting his poetical house in order. That year they had hoped to come back to England, but lack of money forbade even a summer holiday in the mountains. In the winter that followed Elizabeth had the worst chest attack that she had experienced in Italy; the complaint which had once confined her to her couch had recurred only infrequently since her marriage, but she had always to husband her strength. By the summer of 1855, however, she was well again and anxious once more to visit England. The *Men and Women* was finished but for the dedication, which was written later in their London lodgings. In London once more there were countless social engagements, with Ruskin, Leighton, Carlyle, Kinglake, Forster, the Kemble sisters, Russell Lowell and the Proctors. On one occasion Tennyson and Rossetti called at once, and the Dorset Street lodgings witnessed the meeting of four of the age's chief poets. It was a splendid occasion. Tennyson recited his still unpublished *Maud*, Browning, who was generally shy of public performances, read 'Lippo Lippi,' while Rossetti, in a corner, made a rapid pen and ink sketch of Tennyson, which he presented to Browning as he left. Later Browning sat to him for a portrait. Then when the proofs of *Men and Women* were corrected and London began to feel the first chills of autumn, the Brownings left once more for Paris.

Gay though their summer had been, one incident had come very much to disturb Robert Browning's peace if mind. For in London Elizabeth's interest in spiritualism, which had received such poor sustenance around the disappointingly stolid table at Casa Guidi, was rewarded by far more spectacular phenomena produced under the inspiration of the American medium Daniel Home. Home and spiritualism were already the rage in fashionable society. But at the first séance he attended Browning asserted that he had caught Home cheating. The idea of communication with the dead, however, had seized strongly on Elizabeth's imagination. She had been enquiring for years from all her friends about spiritualistic manifestations in London, New York and Paris; now for the first time she could witness them. Perhaps after her husband's outburst she was a little less uncritical, but she did not accept his view of Home. She was much hurt in fact when he showed that adventurer the door on the occasion of his calling at Dorset Street. Her belief was not perhaps dependent on the honesty of any particular medium. She had no liking for Home as a man, and indeed wrote later that she was 'disappointed about him,' conjuring up in the same letter to her sister the pleasant vision of the conjugal furniture floating about his room on his bridal night. But she believed most strongly in the truth of spiritualistic doctrine, which she held to be a vital proof of the unseen world offered to a materialistic age. On this matter Robert and Elizabeth continued to differ; it was perhaps their only strong difference of opinion in their wedded life. It was not until after her death that Browning published his attack upon Home, which he entitled 'Mr. Sludge the Medium'; and by the time that he wrote it he was prepared to let his victim put up a defence as strong but not as valid as Blougram's. Some of his readers indeed even supposed the poem to be stating some sort of case for the spiritualists, but that it was not.

In Paris, where Elizabeth had been working on her

poem *Aurora Leigh* while Robert made a further vain endeavour to simplify the recalcitrant *Sordello*, she fell ill again; and no sooner had she recovered than bad news came from England, of the serious illness of their old friend John Kenyon. It was to his offices that they owed their original introduction, and to him too they owed most generous financial help. To England therefore they returned, to stay with him for the last time. On his death in the following winter he left each of them a generous legacy.

The first news that greeted them on their return to Florence for the next winter was of the immediate success of *Aurora Leigh*, a success infinitely greater than that of *Men and Women*. Browning had, however, no spice of jealousy in his composition. Probably he still thought that she was really a better poet than he. Indeed he glowed in his wife's fame, and was continually bringing up good reviews of her poem to show to friends, and recounting the editions that had gone through the press.

Now the Brownings planned to visit Egypt and the Holy Land in the next winter, but Elizabeth's health would not allow it. News that her father had died, still unreconciled to her, had greatly distressed her in the spring of 1857. That summer they joined Browning's father and sister on the French coast, staying in Paris on the way, where they met old friends and Browning gave up writing for a while to try his hand at drawing. Next winter they were again in Rome. Now, in 1859, there were renewed prospects of Italy's unification. All Elizabeth's hopes were pinned on Napoleon III, in whom she unswervingly believed. Robert, as ever, was less credulous, though until the French emperor abandoned the Italian cause when it was half won, taking Savoy and Nice for his reward, he was almost prepared to subscribe to his wife's overestimate of the pocket Napoleon. The news of the peace of Villafranca disillusioned him and brought on a severe attack of Elizabeth's chest complaint, which was rendered more severe by the pains of angina; and, in the midst of his anxiety, Browning assumed responsibility for the aged Landor, who had returned after many years of estrangement to rejoin his family at Fiesole and, after quarrelling with them, found himself homeless.

Next summer the Brownings spent at Siena, with Elizabeth still in an extremely weak condition. There they met the Storys, who had now taken charge of Landor; there, whilst Italy was still in upheaval, Landor wrote alcaics by turns against his wife and against Napoleon III; there Elizabeth Browning corrected the proofs of her *Poems before Congress*, which were still full of uncritical praise of the Emperor, and there, in the evenings they and all their circle sat on their lawn under the ilexes and cypresses, talking over their tea until long after the cool night had fallen, of their hopes and their fears for the new Italy, which was still to be long in taking shape.

Browning at that time proposed to anatomize Napoleon III in a poem, as he was to anatomize that other charlatan Home, about whom he differed so radically with his wife. But *Prince Hohenstiel-Schwangau, Saviour of Society* was not to be published for another twelve years, by which time the Emperor had finally lost his throne and what remained of his reputation at Sedan. Perhaps in the interval that plan of the poem underwent revision; perhaps the pocket Napoleon was allowed to put up a better defence for himself in 1871 than he would have been allowed in 1859.

In the autumn of the next year the Brownings were once more in Rome, and it was here that Elizabeth received news of her sister Henrietta's death. When she had heard that Henrietta was ill she had hoped to go to England, but she had not the strength. Yet Browning was not more than usually apprehensive about her health. Indeed he was enjoying a typical Roman winter. He had laid his writing aside, and in intervals between entertainments was learning to sculpt in Story's studio. He had written nothing, indeed, for a year. The news of Garibaldi's success in Naples and Sicily was encouraging, and on a wave of optimism the Brownings were soon discussing the possibilities of a grand meeting in France that summer with Robert Browning senior, the poet's sister and Elizabeth's sister Arabella. But shortly before their return to Florence, Elizabeth fell ill once more, and all they could do was to get back to Casa Guidi. Now the political news was bad, and this affected the sick woman's spirits. But no one suspected that she was so near her end. On June 28th, however, after less than a week's renewed illness, with almost no presentiment and little pain, Elizabeth Barrett Browning suddenly died, leaving her husband after fifteen years of marriage to face a further twenty-eight years of life alone.

Chapter Five

THE ROUGH ORE ROUNDED

'My life is fixed and sure now,' wrote Browning to his sister in the letter in which he described Elizabeth's last days and her death, 'I shall live out the remainder in her direct influence, endeavouring to complete mine, miserably imperfect now, but so as to take the good she was meant to give me . . . I shall live in the presence of her, in every sense, I hope and believe—so that so far my loss is not *irreparable*—but the future is nothing to me now, except in as much as it confirms and realizes the past . . . I do not feel paroxysms of grief—but as if the very blessing she died giving me, insensible to all beside, had begun to work already.' The remainder of Browning's life was passed in the endeavour to live up to the experience of that moment, and all that is important in his later poetry is the record of his success or failure in his endeavour to do so. Immediately he left Florence with his son, first to join his father and sister on the French coast and then to return to England. He felt that he had no longer any business in Italy, now that she was dead. In London he would be near her sister Arabella; in London Penini could be educated; in London the poetry Elizabeth had left behind her could be published, and his own work (still without *Pauline*) collected in a definitive edition of three volumes.

In the summer of 1862 Robert Browning took a house in Warwick Crescent, Paddington, and was soon being entertained by the very wide circle which he had gathered around him in the past, and which was constantly increased by fresh acquaintances or by the arrival in London of friends whom he had made abroad. His life was for very many years one of ceaseless activity rendered possible only by his buoyant good health. He wrote, he saw his friends, he varied his year by taking long summer holidays at different seaside places on the Breton and Norman coasts. It was the life of a public man, kept in balance by the cult he made of preserving intimacy with Elizabeth's closest friends, with her sister Arabella until her death, with Miss Isa Blagden, with whom he exchanged letters written by her regularly on the 12th of each month, the date of his wedding, and replied to by him on the 19th, and with the Storys. But his greatest responsibility to her memory was the education of their son, which proved no easy task, and over the details of which he brooded with a more than paternal solicitude.

It was not until 1864 that the poet published the successor to *Men and Women*, his small volume of *Dramatis Personae*. The new poems broke no fresh ground. Compared with his *Men and Women* they depended rather more uniformly on the objective anecdote; there were no such pure inspirations as 'Childe Roland.' The most substantial, indeed, of the new monologues, 'Mr. Sludge, the Medium,' adhered very closely to certain recent events, for in it the spiritualist Home, in the very thinnest of disguises, was allowed to attempt not so much his own defence as justification, which took the form of a bitter and penetrating attack on the credulous society people who had encouraged him and his frauds. The poem has the flatness of 'Bishop Blougram' but not the same humanity. For the meanness which in 'Blougram' had been reserved for the interviewing journalist was here the main strand in the character of Mr. Sludge himself. It is stated in the opening lines:

> Now, don't, sir! Don't expose me! Just this once!
> This was the first and only time, I'll swear,—
> Look at me,—see, I kneel,—the only time,
> I swear, I ever cheated—yes, by the soul
> Of Her who hears—(your sainted mother, sir!)
> All, except this last accident, was truth—

From the outset we are debarred from sympathy with this whining, fraudulent creature who preyed on the weaknesses of his clients, but struck treacherously whenever he thought he could catch anyone at a disadvantage. For all the other personages in the great monologues Browning will play the part of defence counsel; but against Sludge he appears in person briefed for the prosecution, thus revenging himself at leisure for the deceptions Home had practised on his dead wife. Caliban, too, mocking, fearing and scolding his god Setebos by turns, is ugly as the personages of *Men and Women* were not. Yet he is inhuman rather than mean, the incarnation of what man would be without love, a creature of primitive intelligence and crude urge for power, creating his deity by the light of his own limitations. There is a deliberate oafishness about his ungainly lines, whose accents are thrown hither and thither in imitation of the slow, jolting action of the creature's mind. Yet Caliban is almost redeemed by his wry humour, and by the native poetry with which he describes the denizens of his isle:

> Yon otter, sleek-wet, black, lithe as a leech;
> Yon auk, one fire-eye in a ball of foam,
> That floats and feeds; a certain badger brown

> He hath watched hunt with that slant white-wedge eye
> By moonlight; and the pie with the long tongue
> That pricks deep into oakwarts for a worm,
> And says a plain word when she finds her prize . . .

Caliban is alive. Mr. Sludge alone is unrelievably drab. Better a savage who knows no god, Browning seems to say, than one who traffics meanly in evidences.

The *Dramatis Personae*, as a whole, is more forthright in tone than *Men and Women*. On the one hand, there are more pieces concerned with human baseness; on the other, at least five poems make greater affirmations of spiritual truth than their more oblique predecessors, 'The Epistle of Karshish,' and 'Cleon.' The least interesting pieces in the new book are a group concerned with life's seamy side, poems for the most part dwelling on love's decay, and ascribing its cause rather to the shortcomings of the lovers than, as in earlier poems of love and loss, to the contrariness of circumstance.

> I had dipped in life's struggle and, out again,
>   Bore specks of it here, there, easy to see,
> When I found my swan and the cure was plain;
>   The dull turned bright as I caught your white
> On my bosom: you saved me—saved in vain
>   If you ruined yourself, and all through me!

It was a vein that was to be worked more succinctly by Thomas Hardy who, lacking belief in an ideal of behaviour from which his characters had fallen, was able to present their circumstances more barely, and to suggest a more potent and indifferent destiny than Browning believed in. Unsuccessful though 'May and Death,' 'Apparent Failure,' and two or three more pieces were, they at least prepared the way for the later poet's more astringent treatment of Life's little ironies.

How many of the *Dramatis Personae* were written before Elizabeth's death there is no means of knowing. Most, however, must have been the product of the poet's early months in London. Indeed, the triumphant unstopping of the full organ, the blaring out of the mode Palestrina in 'Abt Vogler,' 'Rabbi ben Ezra,' 'Prospice' and the 'Epilogue' may well be read as evidences that Browning was indeed beginning to live on in the spirit of his letter to his sister, written after Elizabeth's death; 'living on in the presence of her, in every sense.' For in the person of his learned Hebrew, ben Ezra, he returns once more to the mood of 'Saul,' this time affirming that old age is, as it was in a more limited sense for his grammarian, the fulfilment of life, and proclaiming afresh that sublime resolution of the world's dichotomy that he had reached in 'Saul.' 'Should not the heart beat once "How good to live and learn",' asks the old rabbi, with deeper wisdom than the plodding grammarian had ever attained.

> Not once beat 'Praise be Thine!
> I see the whole design,
> I, who saw power, see now love perfect too:
> Perfect I call thy plan:
> Thanks that I was a man!
> Maker, remake, complete,— I trust what Thou
>   shalt do!'
>
> For pleasant is this flesh;
> Our soul, in its rose-mesh
> Pulled ever to the earth, still yearns for rest;
> Would we some prize might hold
> To match those manifold
> Possessions of the brute—gain most, as we
>   did best!
>
> Let us not always say
> 'Spite of this flesh today

> 'I strove, made head, gained ground upon the
>   whole!'
>   As the bird wings and sings,
>   Let us cry 'All good things
> Are ours, nor soul helps flesh more, now,
>   than flesh helps soul!'

It was a jagged affirmation, one might say, wrung from recalcitrant experience in a struggle which has impressed itself on the uneven texture of the lives. Compared to his own 'Saul' and, even more, when contrasted with Shelley's 'Lines to a Skylark,' a poem not dissimilar in metre and mood, 'Rabbi ben Ezra' seems deliberately rough; the final lines of each stanza appear indeed purposely to hold up the poem's flow, whereas in Shelley's poem they lead smoothly into the next verse. The Rabbi's glorification of old age remained a favourite of Browning's till the last. There was a sense in which he himself had always looked forward to 'the last of life,' as the fulfilment 'for which the first was made;' it was with this thought in mind, perhaps, that he had written off his youth, in that curious letter to Elizabeth in which he had spoken of having his mind 'set in ultimate order for the few years more.' Unlike the Romantics, he had set out from the start to write not the poetry of youth but that of old age. That was why his desire had been to hasten his maturity and transcend with all speed the mood he had expressed in *Pauline*. Therefore it was, in anticipation, that he placed so many of his profoundest poems on the lips of old men.

'Abt Vogler,' the second of the new book's great affirmations, flows more smoothly than 'Rabbi Ben Ezra,' its anapaestic measure suggesting a less impeded optimism than the Hebrew's broken iambics. But its scope is smaller. For the musician, with all his orchestral soaring, is celebrating no more than the C major of *this* life, even though he dwells on the intimations of a deeper reality that come with the practise of art. Ben Ezra, on the other hand, like the David of 'Saul,' completes the triple pattern and proclaims a fuller faith. 'Abt Vogler' might conceivably have been written before Elizabeth's death; 'Ben Ezra' could not have been, for its certainty can only have been plucked from the teeth of dire adversity.

What had been discursive thought in *Christmas Eve and Easter Day* and what had been oblique and objective in the 'Epistle of Karshish' were combined, in the new book, in a single monologue that is perhaps the greatest of all. 'A Death in the Desert,' the third of its major triumphs, is written in Browning's familiar, reflective mood. It is one of the most profound statements of the Protestant standpoint in English poetry, for its certainty also has been gained in a struggle, in this case in a struggle against the forces of both dogma and doubt. It is a record of the last days of St. John, dying in some Syrian cave whither he has been transported to avoid the persecutions that are now beginning, of

> brother John,
> Who saw and heard and could remember all . . .

and who knew that if the times were at hand when there would be no more living witnesses to testify to the truth of the Gospel story, the doubt that must now ensue is essential to the Divine purpose. For

> . . . man knows partly but conceives beside,
> Creeps ever on from fancies to the fact,
> And in this striving, this converting air
> Into a solid he may grasp and use,
> Finds progress, man's distinctive mark alone,
> Not God's, and not the beasts': God is, they are,
> Man partly is and wholly hopes to be.

The Rough Ore Rounded

> Such progress could no more attend his soul
> Were all it struggles after found at first
> And guesses changed to knowledge absolute,
> Than motion wait his body, were all else
> Than it the solid earth on every side,
> Where now through space he moves from rest to rest.

This is the clearest statement of Browning's belief in all his poetry, a statement the more solemn for the flatness of its imagery, and by the mere hair's breadth that it rises above the prose of that scientific materialism which it so triumphantly refutes. It was such a statement that Tennyson felt empowered to make in his moments of spiritual experience, but which he could never substantiate in poem or discussion. Perhaps Browning owes some of his contemporary unpopularity to his defence of just this pedestrian belief that doubt is far from being the virtue that it is at present assumed to be, that it is a state to be transcended and that God's great gift to man is that he should conceive of truth,

> And yearn to gain it, catching at mistake,
> As midway help till he reach fact indeed.

Dramatis Personae met, on its publication, a far greater measure of success than had any previous book of Browning's. A second edition was soon in the press. For a new generation was growing up for whom the difficulties of his poems seemed to have diminished. It was particularly in the University towns of Oxford and Cambridge that sales were high. But not only was Browning finding new readers among undergraduates; soon his poetry was to find critics in England as penetrating as his friend Milsand in France. Three years after the appearance of *Dramatis Personae* both Edward Dowden his future biographer, and F. J. Nettleship were re-examining *Sordello* and proclaiming that its obscurities were not so great after all. But by this time Browning was at work on that masterpiece that took him four years to write, *The Ring and the Book*.

The tale of Browning's discovery and purchase of the square yellow book containing the story of a Roman murder which had been the sensation of the year 1698 is told in the first book of the poem itself. It was on a torrid June day in 1860 that he picked it up for a mere lira in the square of San Lorenzo in Florence, and began to read it before he had left the market, continuing in the words of the poem itself,

>   from written title-page
> To written index, on, through street and street,
> At the Strozzi, at the Pillar, at the Bridge;
> Till by the time I stood at home again
> In Casa Guidi by Felice Church,
> Under the doorway where the black begins
> With the first stone-slab of the staircase cold,
> I had mastered the contents, knew the whole truth
> Gathered together, bound up in this book,
> Print three-fifths, written supplement the rest.
> *Romana Homicidiorum*—nay,
> Better translate—'A Roman murder-case:
> Position of the entire criminal cause
> Of Guido Franceschini, nobleman,
> With certain Four the cutthroats in his pay,
> Tried, all five, and found guilty and put to death
> By heading or hanging as befitted ranks,
> At Rome on February Twenty Two,
> Since our salvation Sixteen Ninety-Eight:
> Wherein it is disputed if, and when,
> Husbands may kill adulterous wives, yet 'scape
> The customary forfeit.'

The Rough Ore Rounded

At a cursory reading Browning 'knew the whole truth.' The yellow book contained no obliquities. There was no doubt from the start about the innocence of the murdered wife. All the pleadings and counter-pleadings were there, all the depositions of defendants and witnesses, everything but the mystery of human motive and the convolutions of human character which were to be the true subject of his poem when it came to be written. The book immediately seized upon Browning's imagination, and he began to outline a poem which should view these events, now more than a century and a half old, from a variety of angles. 'When I had read the book,' he told his friend R. Lehmann, 'I went for a walk, gathered twelve pebbles from the road, and put them at equal distances on the parapet that bordered it. Those represented the twelve chapters into which the poem is divided, and I adhered to that arrangement to the last.' But he did not begin the writing of *The Ring and the Book* at this point. For within a few months he was offering the story to one friend as the possible plot for a novel, and later suggesting to another that he should write a historical account of the case. It was not until after the publication of *Dramatis Personae* that he set about collecting further documents concerning this 'Roman murder' and embarked on his four years' task.

The Ring and the Book was to be his greatest achievement in the field of monologue, for in it nine personages were to reveal themselves by casting concentric but contradictory lights on the same events, with the poet speaking in person at the opening and the close. Here the weaknesses that had prevented his writing successful plays were to be turned to strengths, the succession of soliloquies combining to build a mighty drama of a new sort, a drama for the study, it is true, but one in which the greatest issues of good and evil, and all the intervening greys and half-tones between them would take human shape. Here a tenfold soliloquy would be harmonized into a single celebration of woman's innocence and her redemptive purity. From the mingled ore and alloy of that brutal Roman tale was to be shaped a ring. Then by an artificer's trick the impurities required for its forging were to be spirited away under acid, to leave it pure gold. The ring's symbolism was two-fold. It stood for the marriage of Robert and Elizabeth Browning, to the memory of which the whole poem was dedicated. But it stood also for the marriage of fact and fiction, for the 'pure fact' of unalloyed gold that could be extracted from the raw material of life, by use of an alloy, the poetic imagination. The book was the raw material; the ring the refined, delicately incised product, and his supreme tribute to Elizabeth. For in Pompilia, its murdered heroine, he saw, despite her extreme youth, the figure of his dead wife, a figure who for all her everyday tarnished circumstances, strikes the priest Caponsacchi, who is to contrive her rescue, as the symbol of eternal womanhood at the first moment he sees her, there at the window of her husband's house,

> Framed in its black square length, with lamp in hand,
> Pompilia: the same great, grave, griefful air
> As stands i' the dusk, on altar that I know,
> Left alone with one moonbeam in her cell,
> Our Lady of all the Sorrows.

But not only 'Our Lady of Sorrows,' not only Elizabeth Barrett, have gone to Pompilia's composition. She has the childish innocence of Pippa, too, of a Pippa on whom Monsignor has had no mercy,

> a child
> Of seventeen years, whether a flower or weed,
> Ruined . . .

For so she seems to that 'Other Half-Rome,' the spokesman of the gossips who take her part. Certainly Pompilia is a great deal more than the pathetic victim Browning read of in the square yellow book. She is Our Lady of Sorrows, Elizabeth, Pippa and also—the incarnation of selfless love, of that selfless love that Robert Browning had long ago tried to express in 'Cristina,' the love of one content to serve without hope of reward; to submit herself, as the Archbishop bade her, to the duties of a loveless marriage, and to flee from that marriage only at the promptings of a higher duty, for the protection of her unborn child but for no happiness that she can expect for herself. The Pope, indeed, skilled in the secrets of the heart, in whom age has come to irradiate intellect with the light of intuition, an old man 'with winter in his soul beyond the world's,' sees her as the incarnation of that quality which the world so tragically lacks. 'Is man strong, intelligent and good,' he asks, 'up to his own conceivable height'—

> Is there strength there?—enough: intelligence?
> Ample: but goodness in a like degree?
> Not to the human eye in the present state,
> An isoscele deficient in the base.
> What lacks then, of perfection fit for God
> But just the instance which this tale supplies
> Of love without a limit? So is strength,
> So is intelligence; let love be so.
> Unlimited in its self-sacrifice,
> Then is the tale true and God shows complete.

Unable himself to transcend the intellectual sphere of

moral values, with a great deal of Bishop Blougram remaining in his composition, the Pope sees in this humble victim with her icy resolution, the symbol of a *summum bonum*. Perhaps, indeed, his knowledge of her life may be the one experience left him to attain,

> Just the one prize vouchsafed unworthy me,
> Seven years a gardener of the untoward ground.

In defining the Pope's limitations and his apprehension of higher values lying beyond them, Browning was defining his own state in all but his moments of supreme inspiration. Like the old man, he was for the most part confined to the common levels of experience; his highest aim to view the world without partisanship, to study and present the case of each of his *Men and Women*, trying their merits 'with true sweat of soul,' and reluctant to condemn even a Sludge or a Caliban unheard. But there was a poetry more profound than this forensic dramatization; there were moments of vision; and one of these he expressed in Pompilia, the missing base to the isoscele. The comparison brings us back to the triple pattern of art, love and faith which was fundamental to his experience. By her presence—as by David's at the couch of the sick Saul—the objective study of a Roman murder case, in itself as sordid as the history of Sludge's frauds, though by its Italian background more picturesque, was transformed into an affirmation of faith. For it is the motive of faith that is stressed, with a solemnity recalling that of the Invocation to Light in *Paradise Lost*, in Browning's address to 'lyric love, half angel and half bird,' at the conclusion of the first book. These lines are more than a memorial to his dead wife:

The Rough Ore Rounded

> Never may I commence my song, my due
> To God who best taught song by gift of thee,
> Except with bent head and beseeching hand—
> That still, despite the distance and the dark,
> What was, again may be; some interchange
> Of grace, some splendour once thy very thought,
> Some benediction anciently thy smile . . .

Here, and in the Pope's speech, and in the statement of the dying Pompilia lies the core of *The Ring and the Book*. Indeed in Pompilia's conclusion, in the blessing she calls down upon the head of Giuseppe Caponsacchi, Browning rises to a height equal to that of Milton's invocation. In bidding farewell to the priest whose devotion to her has been expressed only in selfless service, she states at the same time Browning's own interpretation—in the spirit of Shelley—of the saying that in heaven there is neither marrying nor giving in marriage. For to him Christ's words were a promise that there exists a link in eternity corresponding to that union which in the realm of time is called marriage. 'Marriage-making for the earth,' he concedes in Pompilia's words,

> With gold so much,—birth, power, repute so much,
> Or beauty, youth so much, in lack of these!

But her dying vision is so acute that she can point to a state transcending it:

> Be as the angels rather, who apart,
> Know themselves into one, are found at length
> Married, but marry never, no, nor give
> In marriage; they are man and wife at once
> When the true time is; here we have to wait
> Not so long neither! Could we by a wish
> Have what we will and get the future now,
> Would we wish aught done undone in the past?

> So, let him wait God's instant men call years;
> Meantime hold hard by truth and his great soul,
> Do out the duty! Through such souls alone
> God stooping shows sufficient of His Light
> For us i' the dark to rise by. And I rise.

It was to Caponsacchi, the worldly priest whom her presence had transformed, that she spoke. Yet the words, if put into the mouth of the dying Elizabeth, might be read as a promise to Browning himself and a reminder of the duty he had still to perform; to hold hard by the truth and, by bearing witness to the light he had known, to shed sufficient of his own for others, if not for her, to rise by.

After Pompilia and the Pope, the characters who stand next in recession from the poem's centre are the two active participants, Caponsacchi himself and the sour, avaricious decayed nobleman, Guido Franceschini, who was her murderer. Franceschini is not a mere Websterian embodiment of perversity, yet there is an Elizabethan quality about him. He has confessed to his crime under torture, but unlike Mr. Sludge he does not whine. He fights back with the cornered doggedness of the impoverished representative of a great line he claims to be. There are indeed moments when he too is invested with a human dignity, moments such as that in which he reasons soberly with his judges, with all the strength of one who has suddenly found a certain clarity:

> Come, I am tired of silence! Pause enough!
> You have prayed: I have gone inside my soul
> And shut its door behind me: 'tis your torch
> Makes the place dark: the darkness let alone
> Grows tolerable twilight; one may grope
> And get to guess at length and breadth and depth.
> What is this fact I feel persuaded of—

The Rough Ore Rounded

> This something like a foothold in the sea,
> Although St. Peter's bark scuds, billow-borne,
> Leaves me to founder where it flung me first?
> Spite of your splashing, I am high and dry!
> God takes his own part in each thing He made;
> Made for a reason, He conserves his work,
> Gives each its proper instinct of defence.
> My lamblike wife could neither bark nor bite . . .

His moment of recollection is over; the poison rises once more to his lips. But now he is not despicable; worthless, greedy, envious, embittered, murderous though he is, something has grown in him under the weight of his suffering. Is it the radiance of the lines he is given to speak, or the unquestioning forgiveness of his 'lamblike' wife that has brought it out? From an Elizabethan villain he has become a sinner whose soul may yet be saved. For, in Browning's eyes, no character was evil beyond redemption, and contrasted though Franceschini is with Caponsacchi, both are, in the ultimate, worldlings who are redeemed by Pompilia: Caponsacchi from a successful but wasted life, and Franceschini from damnation.

The transformation wrought in the ambitious priest by his first snatched interview with her is expressed in the language of a miracle:

> In rushed new things, the old were rapt away;
> Alike abolished—the imprisonment
> Of the outside air, the inside weight o' the world
> That pulled me down. Death meant, to spurn the
> > ground,
> Soar to the sky,—die well and you do that.
> The very immolation made the bliss;
> Death was the heart of life, and all the harm
> My folly had crouched to avoid, now proved a veil
> Hiding all gain my wisdom strove to grasp.

It was not the flowering of love, but an experience akin to the birth of faith in one whose religion had been but a formal practice. Franceschini's transformation, on the other hand, comes to him only when in his last despairing cry he utters her name:

> Abate,—Cardinal,—Christ,—Maria,—God, . . .
> Pompilia, will you let them murder me?

The remaining five sections of the book are given up to opinion and commentary, which serve the purpose of revealing the complexities of the case, of giving the drama body and background, and of acting as a kind of obscene chorus of the blind, probing and poking at the wonder they cannot see. Pompilia's innocence indeed appears the whiter for its handling and mishandling by one half-Rome and the other, and by that judicious third personage, neutral, flippant and indifferent, who sums the matter up for some Highness or Excellency, and in fact gives as objective a view of the matter—for all that it is worth—as anybody concerned with the case. Then there are the lawyers, Juris Doctor Johannes Baptista Bottinius, who succeeds in smirching Pompilia as much by his compromising defence as does his pedantic colleague, the excellent Latinist Dominus Hyacinthus de Archangelis, by his assumption of her adultery. The whole motley assemblage is brought to life by the vigour and subtlety of Browning's verse; the courtroom is full; and Rome and Arezzo and Florence, the scenes of the drama, palpitate with noisy, argumentative passions. In 'Mr. Sludge' and 'Bishop Blougram,' Browning's line has shown signs of a certain drabness, the usual concomitant with him of an English subject. *The Ring and the Book*, however, true to its setting, took on the far greater colour of his earlier Italian poems; indeed it contains the very best and subtlest of Browning's blank verse. Nowhere more than here was he the master of variety within a uniform pattern. Other poets in as long a narrative might have resorted to metrical variations, but Browning was able to make each character speak in his own idiom within the limits of a single verse form. There is the broken, nervous defence of de Archangelis, whose mind is half on the case and half at home, where they are preparing a party for his young son. He can have little sympathy with the violence and wounded pride of his client Guido Franceschini, but he makes an eloquent pleading. His opponent Bottinius, on the other hand, puts up a far more rhetorical display, at the expense of Pompilia whose good name he should be trying to preserve. Nothing of this is superfluous. To reduce the poem, as many have wished to, by the five chapters of commentary and pleadings would be to deprive it of its frame. For it is the story of a miracle that happened in the world, a miracle all the more compelling because its witnesses did not cease their worldly activities for it, but continued to be the gossips, the casuists, the sycophants they had always been.

It has been objected, of course, that so commonplace an incident as that recorded in the square yellow book is too trivial a subject for great poetry. Wonder has been expressed that Browning should take such a great interest in murder trials. For, like his father before him, he was minutely familiar with every *cause célèbre* within living memory. Nor was this the only anecdote of its kind that was to give him the idea for a poem. A partial explanation of their fascination for him lies in the sheer wealth of detail a court case offers. He is the poet, above all others, who revels in documentation. In his poems places are exactly described; animals, vegetation, weather and clouds are exactly recorded. But he had a profounder reason for his concern with the violences and the subtleties of criminal behaviour. It is on a world full of life and contradictory activity that he believed the lightning flash of revelation would strike. As in a picture where crowds rush hither and thither about their own business while the procession of the Cross passes almost unnoticed towards Calvary, so in a courtroom and a city, preoccupied with the scandal of a *cause célèbre*, the miracle of its central figure is hardly observed. Violence attracted Browning both as a contrasting background and as a catalyst for the beauty he set out to record.

The reviews of *The Ring and the Book* were uniformly favourable. Never had Browning met with such unstinted praise. It passed immediately into a second edition, and what Mrs. Orr has called the fullest decade of Browning's life began, a decade not only productively rich but one filled with even more social activites. In 1867 Oxford had conferred on the poet an honorary M.A. A little later Jowett was instrumental in getting him elected honorary fellow of Balliol. Next year he was proposed as Rector of St. Andrews, but declined. He feared that the office would entail too much expense. All these honours gave him very great pleasure, for he had long laboured under the feeling that he was neglected, if not openly disliked, by his contemporaries. Not so long ago he had described himself to Mrs. Millais—Ruskin's Effie Gray—as the most unpopular poet that ever was. Now he was coming into his own.

Balaustion's Adventure, published two years after the completion of *The Ring and the Book*, was intended in the first place to be a mere transcript from the *Alcestis* of Euripides, which had been suggested to the poet as a subject by Countess Cowper. Browning had been a

The Rough Ore Rounded

constant reader of Euripides for many years, and was greatly interested in problems of translation. While engaged in this project he discussed many lines in detail with Jowett. But he was not content, as he was to be in later years when he undertook the *Agamemnon* of Aeschylus, merely to give an English version of the Greek play. There is a passage in Plutarch's life of Nicias in which he tells of the welcome given by the Syracusans to Athenian slaves and fugitives who could recite the verses of Euripides, instancing 'a reporte made of a ship of the city of Caunus, that on a time being chased thither by pyrates, thinking to save themselves within their portes, could not at the first be received, but had repulse: howbeit being demaunded whether they could sing any of Euripides songes, and answering that they could, were straight suffered to enter, and come in.' On this ship Browning places his Rhodian girl, Balaustion, who by reciting the *Alcestis* and describing its actions wins a reception for her countrymen and a husband for herself.

By this oblique method of presentation Browning was able to graft upon Euripides' play an interpretation of his own. For the legend of Alcestis had significances that applied to his own case. There was a parallel, as he saw it, between his own loss of Elizabeth and the widowed condition of Admetus, whose wife had gone down into Hades, leaving him 'with her whole soul entered into his.' Such an idea of a mingling of souls was Shelleyan, though perhaps Platonic in its first origins, and certainly foreign to Euripides' way of thought. This did not prevent Browning from introducing it into Balaustion's commentary on the action, and with it another interpretation of his own, also unvouched for by the Greek original. For in *Balaustion's Adventure* it is Love, and not

Hercules, who wrestles with death for Alcestis, and brings her back to her husband in the upper world. Furthermore Browning puts into the mouth of Apollo a magnificent speech in praise of the things of this world, which is a pure statement of the poet's own feelings, His feelings also dictate the form of Admetus' speech over his dead wife, into which Browning puts all his own grief and resignation:

> Since death divides the pair,
> 'Tis well that I depart and thou remain
> Who wast to me as spirit is to flesh,
> So thou, the spirit that informed the flesh:
> Let the flesh perish, be perceived no more,
> Bend yet awhile, a very flame above
> The rift I drop into the darkness by.

Balaustion's Adventure is a reconstruction almost Pre-Raphaelite in its patient detail, yet it is less pedagogically accurate than Browning's first attempt in this vein, 'Artemis Prologizes,' for it is informed with far deeper emotion. Not only has the legend of Alcestis a private significance for the poet. It stands also, in the form that he gives it, as a parable telling of personal salvation by the double forces of love and the creative powers, an idea which had been present in so many of his earlier poems, and which his oblique method of presentation allowed him to show here working on various levels.

The colour of the poem is not Greek, but of the nineteenth century. Admetus' action in accepting Alcestis' sacrifice is excused and explained, not by the fact that he was obeying the instructions of Apollo, but by his promise to remain faithful to Alcestis after her death and to take no other wife: a justification very far from the spirit of Euripides. There is, moreover, despite the circumstantial way in which Balaustion tells her story, an air of retrospect about Browning's evocation of the Greek scene. There are passages in which he seems to recall rather the timeless world of art evoked by Keats than the spectacle of a Greek play performed in a Greek theatre which they are intended to portray. The description of Alcestis' funeral, in particular, has clear affinities with the *Ode on a Grecian Urn*, whose lines it seems to echo.

> Wherewith, the sad procession wound away,
> Made slowly for the suburb sepulchre.
> And lo,—while still one's heart, in time and tune,
> Paced after the symmetric step of Death
> Mute-marching, to the mind's eye, at the head
> O' the mourners—one hand pointing out their path
> With the long pale terrific sword we saw,
> The other leading, with grim tender grace,
> Alkestis quieted and consecrate,—
> Lo, life again knocked laughing at the door!
> The world goes on, goes ever, in and through,
> And out again o' the cloud. We faced about,
> Fronted the palace, where the mid-hall-gate
> Opened—not half, nor half of half, perhaps—
> Yet wide enough to let out light and life,
> And warmth and bounty and hope and joy, at once.

So, as in *The Ring and the Book*, life goes boisterously and carelessly on, heedless of the private grief or the sudden miracle in its midst. Alcestis is dead, and the visiting Hercules must be welcomed; tragedy must be hidden from those who are too obtuse to comprehend it.

After the Mediterranean clarity of *Balaustion's Adventure*, its successor, *Prince Hohenstiel-Schwangau, Saviour of Society* seems doubly drab and confused. It is the defence of Napoleon III that Browning had sketched out in Elizabeth's lifetime, but which was not written and published until 1871, the year after the pinchbeck Emperor's eclipse at Sedan. There is something of the spirit of Sludge about this imaginary German princeling who acts as so fictitious a mouthpiece for the exiled Bonaparte. Indeed at the opening of his monologue he is made to voice the fear that his exploits may be compared with the 'stilts and tongs and medium-ware' of the despised Home. But Browning did not view his subject with the undivided hostility he had devoted to Sludge. At his most judicious, he saw the fallen Emperor as one who had, for a time, done genuine service to France and to the world, by standing in the way of those utopian schemes that he so much distrusted. Napoleon III had wished to build on sound foundations, and to that extent Browning could approve of his policies, but fundamentally he found the Bonapartist adventurer unsympathetic. 'I thought badly of him at the beginning of his career, *et pour cause*,' he wrote to Miss Blagden after the poem's publication: 'better afterwards on the strength of the promises he made, and gave indications of intending to redeem. I think him very weak in the last miserable year.' But, only three months before, he had written with uncharacteristic prejudice that Napoleon III should be blotted out of the world as the greatest failure on record, the alleged benefits of his reign being no more than the extravagant interest which a knavish banker pays you for some time, till one fine day he decamps with the principal. A poem written in so divided a mind could be no more than an intellectual exercise. So obscure was its moral indeed that the critics, who were now far from hostile, could not make out whether it was meant as 'a scandalous attack on the old constant friend of England,' or as a eulogium on the Second Empire. It was, of course, neither, though

The Rough Ore Rounded 127

its implications were clearly rather on the side of hostility than of partiality. Even so, Browning had to deny to so intimate a friend as Miss Edith Story that he had 'taken the man for any Hero.' Like other poems whose characters were unsympathetic to the poet, it lacks those touches of natural detail which relieve even the most casuistical of Browning's arguments. The tangled reasoning and the flatness of the verse merely reflected the mediocrity of the Prince whose motives the poet had set out to justify. Compared with the least colourful character in *The Ring and the Book*—Juris Doctor Johannes Baptista Bottinius perhaps—Prince Hohenstiel-Schwangau was disappointingly grey. The poem was far less compelling than any part of Browning's masterpiece. Yet even the monologue of that dubious Saviour of Society contributes features of its own to Browning's self-portrait.

Certainly it provides one more proof, if proof be necessary, of Browning's indeterminate political position. It is a study rather in human motive than in statecraft. Yet its prevailing tone is so far from liberal that it raises doubt as to the genuineness of the liberalism the poet professed. For if the poem has any fixed standpoint it is a preference for the stubborn and muddled conversation of the imperfect and a mistrust for liberal or republican reformism, which seemed to Browning dangerous and chimerical. So at least he states through the mouth of his Prince in what is the core of his defence:

> I saw that, in the ordinary life,
> Many of the little make a mass of men
> Important beyond greatness here and there;
> As certainly as, in life exceptional,
> When old things terminate and new commence,
> A solitary great man's worth the world.

> God takes the business into his own hands
> At such time: who creates the novel flower
> Contrives to guard and give it breathing-room:
> I merely tend the corn-field, care for crop
> And weed no acre thin to let emerge
> What prodigy may stifle there perchance . . .

Though it may be argued that here Browning is speaking only for a character, and a character indeed who admits that there are moments in the world's history when his timid conservatism is not enough, nevertheless, as his intimate friend Mrs. Sutherland Orr remarks in her *Handbook*, the imaginary speaker here so resembles Mr. Browning himself that we forget for the moment we are not dealing with him. The tergiversations of his Prince may not be Browning's, but this statement of belief certainly is. Never since his abandonment of his Shelleyan enthusiasms had he been a liberal in domestic politics in any respect other than his passionate advocacy of the right of free criticism. Abroad, however, like most enlightened men of his day, he sympathized with the Italians in their struggle for unity, and with the North against the South in the American civil war. But this was ground common to both parties, a mere desire to extend to less fortunate lands the benefits of nationalism and unrestricted trade on which England was prospering. Late in life he composed a sonnet proclaiming 'Why I am a Liberal,' but he never found a place for it in his collected work. For by the time of its writing he had already differed with Gladstone over the subject of Home Rule, and was moving in a liberal-unionist direction. In the spring of 1888, meeting the liberal leader at John Murray's, he was somewhat unhappy at being put beside him. Nobody, however, he noted, could have been more agreeable.

Prince Hohenstiel-Schwangau is perhaps the most contrived and intellectual of all the great monologues. Moreover it is also the only one to display real falsities of presentation. For the Prince's opening, addressed to a young lady of an adventurous type—as Mrs. Orr puts it—whom he has picked up in Leicester Square, strikes an undignified note that the poem is slow to recover from.

> You have seen better days, dear? So have I—
> And worse too, for they brought no such bud-mouth
> As yours to lisp 'You wish you knew me!' . . .

The lady seems hardly a fitting listener to play Gigadibs to his Blougram. Indeed the personality of his curiously chosen interviewer, 'under a porkpie hat and crinoline,' casts a preliminary aura of doubt on the value of the 'once redoubted Sphynx's' confession. At first he appears to be no more than a seedy political adventurer; only as the poem progresses does it become clear that Browning has endowed him too with some of his own qualities. But the passages in which the poet speaks with his own voice are much outweighed by the poem's inconsistencies, its casuistries and tangled argument.

Prince Hohenstiel-Schwangau is probably the least successful of Browning's mature works. Even in its form it is a belated survival from the period before *The Ring and the Book*. For by grouping his twelve dramatic monologues around the single theme of the Roman murder, Browning exhausted the possibilities of his medium. Now he was to advance by stages to a simple narrative presentation along a single time sequence, the contrasting interpretations of his story's facts being suggested, not by fictional characters, but by the poet himself in the role of commentator. But this increased objectivity in his narration was more than a merely formal development. It marked both a further stage in the autonomy of the work itself, and a weakening of the emotional drive that set it in motion. Browning, in the years following Elizabeth's death, was concerned with the single theme of his fidelity to her memory, and such poems as touch upon this problem—*Fifine at the Fair* in particular—reveal a certain tightening of emotional tension. For the rest, between *Balaustion's Adventure* and the *Jocoseria* volume, only *La Saisiaz*, written under the impact of a friend's sudden death shows traces of deep and personal feeling. The virtues of these works of Browning's maturity are narrative virtues, the poet's individual cast of mind appearing rather in his choice of subjects and treatment than in personal identification with the characters he created. With the rough ore of his experience, which he had rounded in *The Ring and the Book*, he was now content to alloy a less precious metal, but the resulting amalgam nevertheless was capable of taking a very fine polish. Only with the work of his old age, written in the prospect of a death which he did not fear, does the proportion of gold in his metal signally increase.

Chapter Six

SUBJECTS CLASSICAL AND SENSATIONAL

'IN English literature the creative faculty of the poet has not produced three characters more beautiful or better to contemplate than these three,' wrote the 'Edinburgh' reviewer of the Pope, Caponsacchi and Pompilia. 'We must record at once our conviction, not merely that *The Ring and the Book* is beyond all parallel the supremest poetical achievement of our time, but that it is the most precious and profound spiritual treasure that England has produced since the days of Shakespeare.' With such uncompromising praise did the *Athenaeum* greet Browning's great poem. Thus established in popular favour Browning embarked on that period of his life when the emotions of the past fell into retrospect and the prospect of death was still a distant one. Each poem that he wrote was sure of an appreciative welcome. There were still, of course, the persistently uncomprehending: Fitzgerald, for instance, who never could read Browning, and Carlyle who made very little of him, and Connop Thirlwall, Bishop of St. David's, who spoke of the Chinese-like condensation of his style. Tennyson found *The Ring and the Book* full of strange vigour and remarkable in many ways, though he doubted whether it could ever be popular.

Browning's own opinion of Tennyson in the *Idylls of the King* is very clearly stated in a letter to his constant correspondent Miss Isa Blagden dated 'March 22nd. '70,' for the 19th'—the customary monthly letter having been delayed by three days. 'Well, I go with you a good way in the feeling about Tennyson's new book: it is all out of my head already. We look at the object of art in poetry so differently. Here is an Idyll about a knight being untrue to his friend and yielding to the temptation of that friend's mistress after having engaged to assist him in his suit. I should judge the conflict in the knight's soul the proper subject to describe: Tennyson thinks he should describe the castle, and the effect of the moon on the towers, and anything *but* the soul . . . The old Galahad is to me incomparably better than a dozen centuries of the "Grail," "Coming of Arthur" and so on.' Of William Morris's *Earthly Paradise* he speaks in much the same vein. 'The lyrics were "the first sprightly runnings"—this that follows is a laboured brew with the old flavour but not *body*.' Rossetti he viewed with even less favour. 'I have read his poems,' he wrote to Miss Blagden in a letter three months later than that in which he delivered judgment on Tennyson and Morris '—and poetical they are,—*scented* with poetry, as it were—like trifles of various sorts you take out of a cedar or sandal-wood box. You know I hate the effeminacy of his school,—the men that dress up like women,—that use obsolete forms, too, and archaic accentuations to seem soft—fancy a man calling it a lil', lil'es and so on: Swinburne started this, with other like Belialisms—witness his harp-playér etc. It is quite different when the object is to *imitate* old ballad-writing, when the thing might be; then, how I hate "Love", as a lubberly naked young man putting his arms here and his wings there, about a pair of lovers,—a fellow they would kick away in the reality.' It is strange that though the Pre-Raphaelites were among the first admirers of *Men and*

Subjects Classical and Sensational

Women, and though there is much in common between the meticulous detail of such a poem as *Sordello* and the background of a Rossetti painting, difference of temperament should have so blinded Browning to Rossetti's qualities as a poet. His own effect on the younger man's development had been so strong that William Michael Rossetti speaks of Browning 'like the serpent rod of Moses' swallowing up, for a time, all other influences: readers of Rossetti's 'A Last Confession' can see the evidence. Swinburne too was a warm admirer of Browning and in his book on George Chapman went out of his way to defend the elder poet's work against the charge of obscurity, a service which earned him an obviously delighted and somewhat embarrassed letter of thanks. Only Alfred Austin remained permanently hostile. He was for Browning a shadowy and contemptible figure whom he saw behind any anonymous review that was in the least critical. Austin himself denied authorship of several of the severer notices, but was certainly responsible for an attack on *Balaustion's Adventure*, in which he took various lines out of their context as 'specimens of Mr. B's inability to write.' But little by little there were gathering around Browning a small group of scholarly admirers, whose questions about his work and the details of his early life he answered with very considerable patience. There was the young Edmund Gosse, whose interest was finally rewarded by a series of interviews out of which grew an article for an American magazine upon 'The Early Career of Robert Browning,' and H. Buxton Forman, then at work upon his edition of Shelley. Browning's correspondence with him was concerned rather with the Romantic poets, about whom he had information derived from Leigh Hunt, than with his own. Buxton Forman, all the same, showed his admiration of his contemporary by buying the acting manuscript of *Colombe's Birthday*, which Browning had written out for Charles Kean, from Bertram Dobell for £10. Other admirers were Norman MacColl and Dr. F. J. Furnivall, the Shakespearean scholar, who was later to be joint-founder of the Browning Society. He was to prove, however, a rather embarrassing disciple.

Outwardly Browning's life was uneventful. He was continually entertained, staying at a variety of country houses, chiefly with members of the nobility, and returning hospitality only sparely, for his household was not on the scale that permitted of lavish entertainment. From the time of his father's death, his sister Sarianne lived with him; and shared with him his annual holidays on the French coast. Between the pair there was a very close bond of affection. Penini was a source of considerable anxiety to them both. Shortly before his going up to Oxford, his father had spoken of his moral qualities as 'really nearly all I could wish.' He praised him for his 'truthfulness, and deepness of feeling, and firmness of mind.' But before he was nineteen Penini had begotten children on two French girls met upon holidays. He did not fulfil his father's hopes that he would get into Balliol, but was accepted by Christ Church, where according to Alfred Domett, he made his mark 'more by the skill he showed at rowing and billiards than by any success at the University subjects of study.' 'Pen won't work' was his father's comment. Not only was he idle, but his financial demands were considerable. Clearly he was very far from the prodigy that his parents had supposed. He had however some talents as a draughtsman, and on his coming down from Oxford, without a degree, his father packed him off to Antwerp to study painting, a profession in which,

Subjects Classical and Sensational

perhaps thanks to Robert Browning's reputation and backing, he made some beginnings of a success. But in the meantime the necessity of supplying him with sufficient money to live in the way that he expected involved his father in an uncomfortable situation that he was to regret for many years.

Louisa, Lady Ashburton was a young widow of dark and classical beauty, with a considerable fortune. Like her husband's first wife, she had been extremely devoted to Carlyle. 'A rich and generous presence,' Henry James wrote of her, 'that wherever encountered, seemed always to fill the foreground with colour, with picture, with fine mellow sound and, in the part of everyone else, with a kind of traditional charmed, amused patience.' She was warmhearted and demonstrative, and in the set that Browning frequented she and her friend Lady Marian Alford were leading and most lavish hostesses. He had met her first during her husband's lifetime, and had known her for quite six years when some time in 1871 he proposed marriage. A marriage between a widower of fifty-nine and a widow of forty-two could clearly have none of the romance that he had known with Elizabeth. It was, however, perhaps unnecessarily frank of the poet to say as much in making his proposal. For not only did he make it clear that his heart remained buried in Florence, but he added that it was largely for his son's sake that he contemplated the alliance. Lady Ashburton's indignant refusal was hardly unreasonable, but Browning took it extremely hard, forgiving neither her nor himself for the indignity he had suffered. 'I see every now and then that contemptible Lady Ashburton,' he wrote three years later, 'and mind her no more than any other black beetle—so long as it don't crawl up my sleeve.' So savage a remark is out of keeping with Browning's character. Possibly he had been genuinely fond of Lady Ashburton, and the worldly interests to which he had ascribed his proposal were intended chiefly to excuse himself in the eyes of his dead wife; perhaps his exaggerated frankness was mere scruple, intended to prevent all shadow of deception. Seldom had Browning made so seemingly insensitive a gesture in any relationship before. He had indeed no enemies, except for the one or two who quarrelled with him at that point, out of partisanship for Lady Ashburton. Those to whom he volunteered an explanation, however, remained his friends. Moreover, Lady Ashburton seems to have alienated her sympathizers by bursting out 'in all the madness of her wounded vanity,' as Browning put it, into calumnies easy to rebut. Later she appears to have made some attempts at reconciliation, but Browning resisted them.

Miss Isa Blagden continued faithful; with her perhaps his bond was stronger than ever it had been with Lady Ashburton, for she had known Elizabeth. But he did not meet her often, since she still lived in Florence; and there in 1872 she died. The poet had now no link remaining with Italy, but in the same year his old friend Alfred Domett returned from New Zealand after nearly thirty years of absence, and the friendship, which had lapsed, was joyfully renewed. In April of that year Domett noted in his diary, which provides much material for this period of the poet's life: 'Browning tells me he has just finished a poem, the most metaphysical and boldest he has written since *Sordello*. He is very doubtful as to its reception by the public.' The poem was *Fifine at the Fair*, and its difficulties arose from the care with which Browning disguised the actual incidents which had called it into being. For Mrs. Orr it is 'a defence of incon-

Subjects Classical and Sensational

stancy, or of the right of experiment in love.' She even views it as a piece of 'perplexing cynicism.' In fact it is a statement, overcoloured with self-reproach, of the strong pull of the world against a man's fidelity to his marriage; *Fifine at the Fair* is not an account of his affair with Lady Ashburton; there could be nothing in common between the gipsy girl in the circus tent with

> Sunshine upon her spangled hips,
> As here she fronts us full with pose half-frank, half-fierce,

and the society hostess who had refused him her hand. But though Fifine is not related except in the most distant way to the lady whom he had so unsuccessfully wooed, the poem is the direct outcome of his experience with Lady Ashburton. For it had brought sharply to his notice the extent to which the memory of his marriage was growing dim. He was unwilling, however, to symbolize by a woman of flesh and blood, the forces which were deflecting him. That would have been to admit too much. So it was a creature half-girl, half-woman, elusive, strange and almost sexless, that he cast for the role of temptress. Yet even as she is copied from a gipsy seen at a French fair, she does not fail to betray her singular fascination for the lonely widower who created her. The intention of the poem, Browning told Dr. Furnivall, 'was to show merely how a Don Juan might justify himself, partly by truth, somewhat by sophistry.' But, as both Mrs. Orr and Edward Dowden have complained, it is extremely hard to see where, in this poem, truth ends and sophistry begins. In justifying himself to his shadowy wife—or conscience—Elvire, for his pursuit of the gipsy girl, the husband talks of some necessary knowledge that can only be gained from the other sex. Himself he compares in a most involved piece of argument, to the swimmer who in an introductory lyric has caught sight of a butterfly fluttering above the sea; now he lies on the water, his head almost submerged, till suddenly 'sun, sky and air so tantalize!' that he reaches up his arms to the heavens, and sinks. So he must live, he concludes, immersed in the things of the world, but always struggling to reach above them: a situation which Browning works out in this extended simile:

> I liken to this play o' the body,—fruitless strife
> To slip the sea and hold the heaven,—my spirit's life
> 'Twixt false, whence it would break, and true, where it would bide.
> I move in, yet resist, am upborne every side
> By what I beat against, an element too gross
> To live in, did not soul duly obtain her dose
> Of life-breath, and inhale from truth's pure plenitude
> Above her, snatch and gain enough to just illude
> With hope that some brave bound may baffle evermore
> The obstructing medium, make who swam henceforward soar:
> —Gain scarcely snatched when, foiled by the very effort, sowse,
> Underneath ducks the soul, her truthward yearnings dowse
> Deeper in falsehood! ay, but fitted less and less
> To bear in nose and mouth old briny bitterness
> Proved alien more and more . . .

To mix further with the world, then, served the purpose of making the world seem increasingly unbearable; consorting with a hundred Fifines only served to enhance the value set on a single Elvire. Yet Fifine claims to be nothing that she is not, and Elvire owes her beauty to his artist's imagination—a fact that would be truer of a dead wife than of a living one. Again Elvire stands above Fifine, therefore Fifine can give him more of the lowly

Subjects Classical and Sensational

experience he needs. For Elvire may be trusted; Fifine teaches one to take care of oneself. The argument of the poem becomes more and more intricate. Never had Browning so resolutely refused to speak out. Yet its conclusion is perfectly plain. Though he may convince Elvire in argument of the necessity of his meetings with the gipsy girl, one last meeting with her, and his wife will be gone:

> I go, and in a trice
> Return: five minutes past, expect me! If in vain—
> Why slip from flesh and blood, and play the ghost again!

So the poem ends. But in its epilogue the wife who, though betrayed, he has sworn shall suffice, does return as a ghost, and as a ghost prompts Don Juan, now the householder of an empty house, in the writing of his own epitaph:

> 'Help and get it over! *Re-united to his wife*
> (How draw up the paper lets the parish people know?)
> *Lies M., or N., departed from this life,*
> *Day the this or that, month and year the so and so.*
> What i' the way of final flourish? Prose, verse? Try!
> *Affliction sore long time he bore*, or, what is it to be?
> *Till God did please to grant him ease.* Do end!' quoth I:
> 'I end with—Love is all and Death is nought!' quoth She.

Browning remains enigmatically ironic to the end. For the poem's problem is insoluble; nor was he prepared to state it as frankly as he had stated his problems before. There is throughout a confusion that appears almost deliberate about the precise benefits to be won from the alluring gipsy. Was it knowledge that his Don Juan was seeking, or diversion? 'An actual Elvire and an actual Fifine may be the starting points,' writes Dowden, 'but by and by Elvire shall stand for all that is permanent and substantial in thought and feeling,

Fifine for all that is transitory and illusive.' In face of Browning's own statement to Dr. Furnivall, and the knowledge that has transpired about his relations with Lady Ashburton since Dowden wrote, one must conclude that his assessment of the poem is over-philosophical. Its merits lie entirely in its descriptive passages. Seascapes and landscapes evoking the flat country about Pornic, the picture of the fair itself and of the carnival in St. Mark's Square at Venice, go some way towards atoning for the critical disquisitions that obscure but do not conceal the fundamental content of the poem.

Fifine at the Fair is not, for all its narration in the first person, a dramatic monologue. The 'Men and Women' had spoken with their own voices and in their own defence, but the personality of Don Juan in *Fifine* is no sooner created than it disintegrates, leaving Robert Browning with a mere ventriloquist's dummy to speak his reflective discursions. The unfaithful husband is among the poet's very few unsuccessful creations, for soon Browning does not even trouble to fit his language to the probable thoughts and viewpoint of the man who is supposed to be talking. Such were the penalties of his reluctance to speak out.

Fifine at the Fair differs from its predecessors in its metrical form. For Browning was never permanently content with the blank verse medium over which he had won such mastery. The six-beat line of *Fifine*, and its division into short sections corresponding to paragraphs, the reintroduction of rhyme and the frequency of anapaests, seem to blur the poem's argument. Much of it indeed appears to have been composed in an emotional undertone.

In *Red Cotton Night-cap Country*, Browning's next poem, he returned to blank verse, and advanced a stage further towards objective presentation. In this second dramatization of a *cause célèbre*, he touches, perhaps with less reluctance than in *Fifine at the Fair*, on the same problem of self-mastery or self-indulgence, and on yet another of the questions which had exercised him throughout his life, that of belief in the supernatural. In its inception *Red Cotton Night-cap Country* was as deliberate an exercise as *Balaustion's Adventure*. The story of *Fifine at the Fair*, however overstrained, was of the stuff of Browning's own experience. The fascination of a gipsy had long ago promoted 'The Flight of the Duchess' and an actual Fifine had attracted him at an actual fair. *Red Cotton Night-cap Country*, however, owed its origins to a dispute with Miss Annie Thackeray, whom he met at St. Aubin on the Norman coast in the summer of 1872. She had humorously described the district, from the caps of the fisherfolk as 'White Cotton Night-cap Country.' Everything was so sleepy, she implied, that nothing at all ever happened there. Browning however knew of certain melodramatic happenings which had taken place in the previous year and which made 'Red Cotton Night-cap Country' a more fitting name for the district. As the poem opens in this meek, 'hitherto un-Murrayed bathing-place' he reasons with Miss Thackeray on the relative suitability of the two titles. The case which Browning interpreted in his poem was in its origins a simple one: a Paris jeweller who had lived with a mistress on a local estate had killed himself by jumping from a tower. In the tale, as told to the poet by his friend Milsand, the reason for his suicide had been remorse at his unfilial behaviour to his mother, and at the grief his irregular union had cost her. Later, however, when Milsand told him more Browning decided that the man's chief considerations had been religious. The accounts he then collected locally and from the newspapers confirmed him in this interpretation. The original Mellerio, a Spaniard, had certainly been a man with a strong vein of superstition in his make-up; Browning, however, saw him, in more extreme terms, as a man who had demanded a miracle. His jumping from the tower had been, as the poet viewed it, no suicide but a challenge to the Virgin of a local church to transport him through the air, a supernatural event which would condone—or even justify—the uneasy compromise between faith and immorality in which he was endeavouring to live. The poem's central theme is the impossibility of this compromise. As it was impossible for the Don Juan of *Fifine at the Fair* to divide his life between Elvire and the gipsy, so the jeweller of *Red Cotton Night-cap Country* is unable to reconcile the 'Turf and Towers' of its subtitle. The two symbols recur in the poem with a constancy unusual in Browning's work, the Tower from which Mellerio's counterpart Léonce Miranda jumps to his death standing for the religious life, and the Turf on which he falls for the life of the world. But the miracle in which the crazy jeweller comes to believe will reconcile this duality and solve everything. Nor will its effects be limited to his own benefit. The news of it will be the signal for the revival of faith throughout France. He imagines Renan coming out into the street where he lives in Paris and burning his book, and Napoleon III, when he hears of it, resigning his Empire, 'twenty years usurped,' to the legitimate Bourbon, 'Henry the Desired One,' who will from that moment reign in France.

> O blessing, O superlatively big
> With blessedness beyond all blessing dreamed
> By man! for just that promise has effect,
> 'Old things shall pass away and all be new!'

Subjects Classical and Sensational

> Then, for a culminating mercy-feat,
> Wherefore should I dare dream impossible
> That I too have my portion in the change?
> My past with all its sorrow, sin and shame,
> Becomes a blank, a nothing!

So, like another Master-builder, he stands in the Belvedere he has himself constructed, ready to take flight; in the Belvedere for whose creation his mother has reproached him, viewing it as the overweening sign of his extravagance. For, as Browning drew her, she had advocated an impracticable, mere easy-going compromise between the twin claims of turf and towers, recommending indeed that he and his mistress should live on quietly in the country, inhabiting no grand new apartments but

> the south room, that we styled,
> Your sire and I, the winter chamber.

Browning departs so far from the story as he had first heard it as to make her underline the moral which he had already stated in his capacity of commentator, that man should climb no towers but pick his way 'like a sage pedestrian.'

But Léonce Miranda is not capable of taking a middle path. Like Ibsen's architect, he has built a tower within himself from which he must challenge, not the future generation that treads him down, but the rising tide of unbelief. But this deed will do more; it will restore the innocence of his smirched mistress. The Virgin will join his hand with hers in true marriage; he will worship one and yet love the other. The poem becomes at this point a crazy travesty of *The Ring and the Book*. It is as if the Pope were asked to give his blessing to the carnal marriage of Caponsacchi and Pompilia.

Not only is Miranda crazy, however, but his tower, the tower of the old faith, cannot be rebuilt. His attempt to raise it in the form of a new Belvedere is as fantastic as his appeal to miracle. Here Browning repeats in stronger form his judgment upon the Church of Rome delivered in 'Christmas Eve':

> Disturb no ruins here!
> Are not they crumbling of their own accord?
> Meantime, let poets, painters keep a prize!

The picturesque towers of the old faith might be the stuff of which poems and paintings could be made, but now there were other paths to tread, and not all of them hugged the flat ground. There was a steadier method of climbing now, the method of utilizing doubt long ago adumbrated by the dying Saint John in 'A Death in the Desert,' and Browning's moral for *Red Cotton Night-cap Country* is in effect a secular restatement of that poem's message that:

> God's gift was that man should conceive of truth
> And yearn to gain it, catching his mistake
> As midway help till he reach fact in deed.

It is a judgment of the same weight that Browning was now delivering, ten years later, in his role of commentator, upon the sordid fate of his crazy jeweller. If you are adventurous and climb yourself, he advises his reader,

> Plant the foot warily, accept a staff,
> Stamp only where you probe the standing point,
> Move forward, well assured that move you may:
> Where you mistrust advance, stop short, there stick!
> This makes advancing slow and difficult?
> Hear what comes of the endeavour of brisk youth
> To foot it fast and easy!

Subjects Classical and Sensational 145

Red Cotton Night-cap Country was condemned by R. H. Hutton of the *Spectator* for containing no single line of poetry. In argument he conceded to Alfred Domett a single passage, which does not today seem to stand out from the even texture of the poem. Certainly it is concerned throughout, except where the poet interpolates a passing sketch of Milsand, with the morally sordid. Moreover it bears marks of hasty writing; it took Browning only seven weeks to complete the first manuscript from which it was printed. Yet, despite a few obscure passages, it makes far easier reading than *Fifine at the Fair*, for the verse, though it does not rise to passages of beauty that would be foreign to the purpose of the poem, very seldom falls into flatness. There are indeed few descents in the course of the whole of the poem's forty thousand lines. Browning certainly remained the master of his medium, and was still a superb analyst of motive, but the world about him was growing dark and he was alone. Yet in the ugliness and evil that seemed everywhere to confront him, he found always reflections of sanity and truth, if not of beauty.

In *Aristophanes' Apology*, however, which followed upon *Red Cotton Night-cap Country* two years later, in 1875, Browning returned to the deliberate pursuit of beauty, taking up the tale of Balaustion where he had left it, and using it as a framework for a transcript this time of the *Heracles* of Euripides. The poem as a whole falls below the level of *Balaustion's Adventure*, being rather an archaeological reconstruction in the manner of the prologue he had once given to Artemis than a poem with deep personal associations. It contains however passages of real magnificence recalling the supreme Miltonic invocations in *The Ring and the Book*, passages the more welcome for the poem's position in Browning's œuvre between *Red Cotton Night-cap Country* and *The Inn Album*. There are few finer affirmations in all his work than Balaustion's on her flight back to Rhodes after the fall of Athens:

> Why should despair be? Since, distinct above
> Man's wickedness and folly, flies the wind
> And floats the cloud, free transport for our soul
> Out of its fleshly durance dim and low—,
> Since disembodied soul anticipates
> (Thought-borne as now, in rapturous unrestraint)
> Above all crowding, crystal silentness,
> Above all noise, a silver solitude:—
> Surely, where thought so bears soul, soul in time
> May permanently bide, 'assert the wise,'
> There live in peace, there work in hope once more—
> O nothing doubt, Philemon! Greed and strife,
> Hatred and cark and care, what place have they
> In yon blue liberality of heaven?

After this the poem's arguments concerning the nature of comedy and the justification for satire seem a little academic. The rest of the verse is clear and good with occasional passages of description as colourful and pleasing as the best in the *Adventure*, but about the whole poem and the *Heracles* translation it contains, clings the air of the study, which was rendered stuffier rather than dispelled by such notes as that informing the reader that the kordax-step was the Greek equivalent of the can-can.

The Inn Album, published in the same year as *Aristophanes' Apology*, draws once more on law reports from the contemporary press. Little though Browning felt in theory that such should be the exclusive subjects of his poems, in this phase of his life they inevitably were. For in this poem, to a greater degree than in *Red Cotton*

Subjects Classical and Sensational 147

Night-cap Country, Browning was obsessed by death. In *The Inn Album* indeed the number of deaths is in excess of the poetic probability. It is perhaps right that the elder woman confronted by her former lover and jolted out of the dead life she had been living, should commit suicide; the murder of that lover by her younger admirer, however, is not very convincing. The characters are right, but the dénouement, owing to Browning's too great addiction to violence, is false. The plot is one of the neatest Browning ever contrived, preserving as it does the unities of time and place. He claimed that it was founded on a story told him thirty years before by Lord de Ros. Whether founded on fact or not, it allowed of far better shaping than had the stuff of *Red Cotton Night-cap Country*. But not only is its story much more compact, it contains also passages of far more concentrated verse than he had written since *Balaustion's Adventure*, among the best a description of a night walk that shows the vigour with which the poet of *Pauline* and *Sordello* lived on in the middle-aged widower who wrote *The Inn Album*:

> 'Twixt wood and wood, two black walls full of night
> Slow to disperse, though mists thin fast before
> The advancing foot, and leave the flint-dust fine
> Each speck with its fire-sparkle. Presently
> The road's end with the sky's beginning mix
> In one magnificence of glare, due East,
> So high the sun rides,—May's the merry month.

But there is no merriment in the hearts of the characters, and the curtain falls on an Elizabethan plethora of corpses upon which an unsuspecting and innocent girl is about to open the door. Edward Dowden compares it with that brief and poignant dramatization of an earlier murder case, the anonymous *Yorkshire Tragedy*. Certainly its colour is a murky grey relieved only by occasional glimpses of the English countryside in which it is set, and by the charm of the younger woman, whose appearances however are few. The inn itself might be situated in Hell so little hope is there for those who enter there; in that Hell which is described by the elder woman's narrow clerical husband, a place where he expects the wicked to meet:

> After death,
> Life: man created new, ingeniously
> Perfect for a vindictive purpose now
> That man, first fashioned in beneficence,
> Was proved a failure; intellect at length
> Replacing old obtuseness, memory
> Made mindful of delinquent's bygone deeds
> Now that remorse was vain, which life-long lay
> Dormant when lesson might be laid to heart. . .

The picture of man granted the power to know the consequences of good and evil only at the moment when it is too late for him to make use of his knowledge is among the ugliest drawn by any nineteenth-century poet, exceeding even the horror of *The City of Dreadful Night* from which, at least, Thomson believed there was release at death. It is indeed strange, in the light of such a passage, that Browning should still be censured for his facile optimism.

Formally *The Inn Album* is the most perfect of the shorter novels in verse. It is also Browning's final achievement in direct narrative of any length, and marks a final peak in the range he had ascended with his *Men and Women*, a range which looks out over a plain which the poet spent the next nine years in crossing. For, except *La Saisiaz*, a poem comparable in its premonitory

Subjects Classical and Sensational 149

significance to *Christmas Eve and Easter Day*, Browning attempted nothing of the first importance thereafter until his not wholly successful *Ferishtah's Fancies* of 1884.

Since the publication of *Fifine at the Fair* the popularity he had won with *Men and Women* and with *The Ring and the Book* had begun to wane. Soon the old reproaches of obscurity began to appear in the journals, though the critics were not so unanimously against him as they had been in the past; the *Athenaeum* reviewer even considered *The Inn Album* an advance upon *The Ring and the Book*. But Browning had long meditated his revenge on the critics, and in his next volume, *Pacchiarotto, and How he Worked in Distemper*, etc., he was to take it. For he had exhausted the vein he had tapped in *Fifine at the Fair* and could now turn his attention to trivial themes. Now the antagonistic pulls of the world and the ideal, the present and the past, were alike growing weaker. Nor did he still think of love as he had done when he wrote *The Ring and the Book*. In *Red Cotton Night-cap Country* it had been no ennobling passion, and the crazy jeweller's endeavour to make it so had preposterously failed. In *The Inn Album* it was a thing of this world only, an obsession that brought grief to its victims, but no intimations of a higher beauty.

In his new lyrical volume Browning treated the subject as he had treated it in early years, in all its possible combinations and situations but without any close reference to his own case. Such poems as 'St. Martin's Summer,' and 'Bifurcation' are studies of cases as imaginary as those of 'A Woman's Last Word' and 'The Last Ride Together.' The *Pacchiarotto* volume, however, was primarily an attack upon the critics, mild and expostulatory in such short pieces as 'House' and 'Shop'—the first of which has been quoted in the opening pages of this study—and rumbustiously offensive in the title poem. For this hasty and deliberately cacophonous attack, which singled out the invidious Alfred Austin for a drubbing, Browning returned to the manner of 'The Pied Piper.' His invective is a little too contemptuous to be amusing, his ingenuity a little too provocative to please. He had treasured up his grievances too long for them to pass as mere good fun. But the lyrics of the new volume, even when using up rags and tags of themes already treated, achieve certain new masteries, chiefly in ironic anecdotes which look forward to Hardy, and in cryptic metaphysical statements that seem directly modelled on the short-lined verse in the second part of *Faust*.

> Could I but live again,
> Twice my life over,
> Would I once strive again?
> Would I not cover
> Quietly all of it—
> Greed and ambition—
> So, from the pall of it,
> Pass to fruition?

This opening of the second of his 'Pisgah Sights' owes everything to Goethe. Yet its claim to compress a lifetime's experience in a few short lines is hardly valid. In fact 'Pisgah Sights' fail to make a statement, chiefly perhaps because Browning was still a long way from having distilled the experience of his life into a single and uniform belief. More typical of his attitude in his sixty-fourth year was his testy demand to be left alone voiced in the poem 'House':

> I have mixed with a crowd and heard free talk
> In a foreign land where an earthquake chanced:
> And a house stood gaping, nought to baulk
> Man's eye wherever he gazed or glanced.

> The whole of the frontage shaven sheer,
>   The inside gaped: exposed to day,
> Right and wrong and common and queer,
>   Bare, as the palm of your hand, it lay.

With Elizabeth's death the front of his house had indeed fallen, and all had been able to witness his sorrow, but now he wished to live on in private without prayers. He did not care to spend the whole of his life publicly selling his wares either, like the poet he writes of in 'Shop,' the companion piece to 'House.' His intention was to withdraw a little and contemplate life's little ironies from a distance. Deliberately he returned to his study, and in 1877 undertook, in order to please Carlyle, a verse translation the *Agamemnon of Aeschylus*. So literal and awkward was this translation that Alfred Domett supposed him intentionally to have made it as difficult for English readers as the original Greek is said to have been for the Greeks. But his drift towards the academic and towards a greater detachment was sharply checked by the death of a very dear friend.

Miss Egerton Smith, whom he had first met in Florence where she had come on a visit, was a wealthy woman of whom he saw increasingly more as his older women friends forsook him. His sister-in-law Arabella, Miss Isa Blagden, Lady Ashburton, all were lost to him by death or difference, and Miss Egerton Smith had come to take their places. With her he went frequently to concerts when in London, and each season for the last few years she had joined the poet and his sister on their various summer expeditions abroad. In the summer of 1877 she was staying with Robert and Sarianne in a small villa called La Saisiaz four or five miles to the south-west of Geneva, when suddenly she died.

'Browning had been for his usual bathe,' wrote Domett in his diary, having heard an account of the matter from Miss Browning, 'in a pool among trees down the mountainside, and on returning found that Miss Smith had not made her appearance. "All right," he thought, "she is saving herself for the journey" (a walk in the mountains which they had planned for that day). Miss Browning going into her room to look for her, found the poor lady lying with her face downwards upon the floor. She put her arm round her, saying, "Are you ill, dear?", then she saw that she was insensible.'

The shock of this sudden meeting with death sent Browning, on his return to London, to re-examine his beliefs once more. In the resulting poem, *La Saisiaz*, his affirmation is less wholehearted than of old, and stronger in its review of the good things of life he had enjoyed than in its statement of philosophical belief. That he trusted in a future life is clear from reports of his conversations with friends. But in *La Saisiaz* he failed to clothe his conviction in striking imagery. The poem's argument is loose and over-wordy; its best lines are not those which testify to his temperate hope of a future immortality, but those which remember the woman who has died, and portray the Alps among which he and she had meant to walk on the day of her death. In places where an emotional clinch is needed, Browning for the first time proves insufficient master of his medium, and lapses into such diffuseness as:

> So, I hope—no more than hope, but hope—no less than hope, because
> I can fathom by no plumb-line sunk in life's apparent laws,
> How I may in any instance fix where change should meetly fall
> Nor involve, by one revisal, abrogation of them all . . .

Subjects Classical and Sensational

Using equally loose metres, Arthur Hugh Clough was able to lend more conviction to his doubts than did Browning to his statement of belief in a future life. Miss Egerton Smith's death had called up a memory, and reminded him of his own mortality. Perhaps it challenged him to look back once more on his own loss. The emotional weakness of much of the poem, however, suggests a refusal to face all its implications. Browning was less ready with answers to his own questions now than he had been when he wrote 'Christmas Eve,' and the only beauties of *La Saisiaz* are the colours of retrospect with which he summons up the vast Swiss landscape:

> There's Salève's own platform facing glory which strikes greatness small,
> —Blanc, supreme above his earth-brood, needles red and white and green,
> Horns of silver, fangs of crystal set on edge in his demesne.
> So, some three weeks since, we saw them: so, tomorrow we intend
> You shall see them likewise; therefore Good Night till tomorrow, friend!

But his friend had not lived to take that walk with its views of Mont Blanc, and Browning was a man of sixty-six who might soon know the answer to the questions his fancy and reason debated in his memorial poem to Miss Egerton Smith.

In his work of the next few years, however, he returned to the lyric and the story. Reflective poetry spoken in the first person he abandoned for ever with *La Saisiaz*. The autobiographical element, nevertheless, was to appear triumphally again.

The Two Poets of Croisic makes a neat juxtaposition of two tales associated with the seaside place where Browning had spent several summers. His first poet,

René Gentilhomme, whose mediocre ode is accepted as a prophecy by the superstitious Louis XIII, subsides into what seems to have been a welcome oblivion; the second poet who has for long believed in his entirely fictitious fame decides in the end that the only true glory is that which a man has had no hand in making. In one sense *The Two Poets* is a premature farewell to Browning's own reputation; what matters, as he sees it, is the experience of being a poet, or of having been a poet. In its modesty, and its treatment only of what Browning has felt and known, the end of *The Two Poets* is more successful that that of *La Saisiaz*. There's a simple test, he says, by which to weigh the worth of poets. The one who prevails will be the

> . . . strong since joyful man who stood distinct
> Above slave-sorrows to his chariot linked.
>
> Was not his lot to feel more? What meant 'feel'
>   Unless to suffer! Not, to see more? Sight—
> What helped it but to watch the drunken reel
>   Of vice and folly round him, left and right,
> One dance of rogues and idiots! Not, to deal
>   More with things lovely? What provoked the spite
> Of filth incarnate, like the poet's need
> Of other nutriment than strife and greed!
>
> Who knows most, doubts most; entertaining hope,
>   Means recognizing fear; the keener sense
> Of all comprised within our actual scope
>   Recoils from aught beyond earth's dim and dense.
> Who, grown familiar with the sky, will grope
>   Henceforth among groundlings? That's offence
> Just as indubitably: stars abound
> O'erhead, but then—what flowers make glad the ground!

Subjects Classical and Sensational

Such verses with their stronger imagery and their closer pattern of alliteration bespeak knowledge greatly in excess of the theoretical philosophizings of *La Saisiaz*. The story of the two poets is pedestrian, but the end of the poem fresh and direct, in its acceptance of the state of doubt which in the earlier poem he had failed to dispel.

The Browning of these late years was an even more solitary man than he had been after Elizabeth's death. Without Miss Egerton Smith he no longer went to concerts. His daily and weekly routine became increasingly rigid. 'He was averse,' writes Mrs. Orr, 'to any thought of change. What he had done once he was wont, for that very reason, to continue doing,' and the way he spent his days was described in detail after his death by an old servant in an article in the *Pall Mall Gazette*.

'He rose without fail at seven, enjoyed a plate of whatever fruit—strawberries, grapes, oranges—were in season; read, generally some piece of foreign literature, for an hour in his bedroom; then bathed; breakfasted—a light meal of twenty minutes; sat by the fire and read his *Times* and *Daily News* till ten; from ten to one wrote in his study or meditated with head resting on his hand. To write a letter was the reverse of a pleasure to him, yet he was diligent in replying to a multitude of correspondents. His lunch, at one, was of the lightest kind, usually no more than a pudding. Visits, private views of picture exhibitions and the like followed until half-past five. At seven he dined, preferring Carlowitz or claret to other wines and drinking little of any. But on many days the dinner was not at home; once during three successive weeks he dined out without the omission of a day. He returned home seldom at a later hour than half-past twelve; and at seven the next morning the round began again.'

It was not a routine conducive to the writing of poetry, but the life of a man who needed human contacts, yet wished to form no new and strong emotional bonds that might cause him to lose his memories of the old ones. Nevertheless in the three hours he spent in his study he composed in the years of his decline the two volumes of *Dramatic Idyls* and *Jocoseria*. The contents of these three books are on a lower level of inspiration than any other group of Browning's poems. Each one of these dozen and a half stories in verse is marred by the Browning mannerisms, and not one of them is brought to life by any urgency in its telling. Monaldeschi's murder fails to arouse the shudder of horror which had been at the poet's command ever since his 'Madhouse Cells'; and 'Ixion' turns on his wheel at no more than a conversational pace. Ned Bratts and his wife brawl excitedly about their conversion, but to no purpose. No reader can care about their fate. The anecdotes might suit a fourteen year old; the method of telling, however, would defeat any but a skilled Browning reader. Here rhymes which had been effective in the aggressive knockabout of *Pacchiarotto* pull the story up short. Nor is Browning any happier in his metres. The six-beat line of *Fifine* takes the place of his characteristic blank verse, and conveys an effect of jocose lightness quite at variance with the poem's purpose. This new awkwardness in Browning's manner bespeaks a growing impatience with anecdote and reader. He will throw his story off as once he threw off 'The Pied Piper,' but now he has lost his skill. Yet among these offhand narratives he dropped occasional short pieces that recalled his long-ago *Dramatic Lyrics*, yet revealed a new art of compression and a live metrical dexterity. Such a piece as 'Never the Time and the Place' amply proves that when

Subjects Classical and Sensational

the old poet was moved he could still write as well as he had done then. Indeed he said as much in his epilogue to the last of the *Dramatic Idyls*:

> Touch him ne'er so lightly, into song he broke:
> Soil so quick-receptive,—not one feather-seed,
> Not one flower-dust fell but straight its fall awoke
> Vitalizing virtue: song would song succeed
> Sudden as spontaneous . . .

But the continued spontaneity of his song could hardly have been credible to those who met him in fashionable drawing-rooms. For the picture that he presented in society was a of rather coarse little man, who was sometimes mistaken for a successful stockbroker. In conversation he was given to the aggressive monologue, often laying down the law on subjects he knew very little about. Politics had by now ceased to interest him, but religious arguments fascinated him, as they did Tennyson. 'Whatever he had to consider or speak about, he disposed of in the most forthright style,' wrote W. M. Rossetti. 'Every touch told, every nail was hit on the head.' Another friend describes him 'as a strong man armed in the completest defensive armour, but with no aggressiveness.' It is difficult, however, to credit him with a permanent absence of aggression; the writer of *Pacchiarotto* was not a man to suffer fools. It is probable that with the years he grew less and less able to allow his fellow guests a hearing. Asked on one occasion whether he did not object to the adulation with which he was treated he replied in surprise: 'Object to it! No; I've waited forty years for it, and now I like it!' 'He appeared,' says Mrs. Orr, 'more widely sympathetic in his works than in his life; with no moral selfishness, he was intellectually self-centred.' Defensive armour is perhaps the most revealing analogy of all. Never to the end of his days was Browning at his ease with his fellow men; always he felt that either by their criticism or their prying they were trying to impinge on his privacy. In private conversation and even in correspondence, he was a great deal more approachable. There exist many of his letters in which he painstakingly explains the meaning of a passage to some correspondent perhaps unknown to him. The stalwarts of the Browning society he treated with ceremonious politeness, which its founder Dr. Furnivall seems to have presumed on. It is seldom perhaps that a scholar has the opportunity of setting an author an examination paper in his own works, and Furnivall certainly took advantage of this privileged situation. Another, even less disinterested, scholar, T. J. Wise, also fastened himself upon Browning with a view to his own profit. Some of his questions in respect to the first publication of such rarities as *Pauline* he was later able to turn to his own dishonest profit. For, some years before his death it was discovered that this assiduous scholar and collector had himself called into existence several 'early' printings of works by the Victorian great. But if the attention of Wise and Furnivall was somewhat self-interested, and if the Browning Society itself was something of an embarrassment, though perhaps an aid to the sale of his books, Browning's friendship with Edmund Gosse had no disadvantageous aspect. It was to Gosse that he handed over the embarrassing box containing the poems and papers of the unfortunate poet T. L. Beddoes, an unwanted legacy, which he had kept for ten years, as Robert Bridges afterwards kept Gerard Manley Hopkins' poems, in doubt as to what he should do with them; and to him he would talk about his own early life and the people he had met. But there is an

Subjects Classical and Sensational 159

occasion recorded by Gosse when Browning launched into a far more exciting topic 'passing from languid and rather ineffectual discussion of some persons well known to us both into vivid and passionate apology for an act of his own Colombe of Ravenstein. It was the flash from conventionality to truth, from talk about people whom he hardly seemed to see to a record of a soul that he had formed and could follow through all the mazes of caprice. It was seldom, even in intimacy I think, that he would talk thus liberally about his sons and daughters of the pen, but that was mainly from a sensible reticence and hatred of common vanity. But when he could be induced to discuss his creations, it was easy to see how vividly the whole throng of them was moving in the hollow of his mind. It is doubtful whether he ever totally forgot any one of the vast assemblage of his characters.' One is reminded of Browning's favourite novelist Balzac, whose characters were more real to him than the men and women he knew.

Gosse had won the old poet's confidence. Usually in society he refused to read his poems or to discuss them. Often he pretended entirely to have forgotten what he had once written. Once indeed he claimed not to have looked at a line of *The Ring and the Book* after it was published. Henry James saw him as a divided personality. The one side which Gosse records, the poet, 'sat at home and knew, as well he might, in what quarter of *that* sphere to look for suitable company.' But the man of the world 'walked abroad, showed himself, talked right resonantly, abounded, multiplied his connections, did his duty.' 'Tennyson,' said some lady, 'hides himself behind his laurels, Browning behind the man of the world.'

In the autumn of 1878, after seventeen years' absence,

the poet went back to Italy, treading once more the streets of Asolo which he had not seen since his earliest visit of all; and from Pippa's town he moved to Venice, where he now stayed each autumn for three years. In England recognition gathered weight. In 1882, Oxford gave him the honorary degree of D.C.L. in celebration of his seventieth birthday, and Edinburgh an LL.D. in 1884. As an outcome of the Browning Society's activities, which in his capacity of a 'new Browningite' he continued to watch with some misgivings—he is said to have asked Gosse not to join it—his old friend Mrs. Sutherland Orr was commissioned to compile her *Handbook to Robert Browning's Works*, a careful piece of exposition, which he characterized in the last year of his life as 'the best of helps for anyone in need of such when reading —or about to read my works. It is done far better than I could hope to do it myself.' It was indeed extremely well done, though not without considerable assistance from Browning himself. Mrs. Orr's interpretations are generally reliable except when she is dealing with Browning's religious beliefs. Here her own theism causes her to underrate his fundamental Christianity. Her *Handbook*, however, which passed through three editions between 1885 and the poet's death, and her biography which appeared in 1891, together with the Browning Society's activities, put the seal on Browning's reputation as poet and philosopher. Whether he subscribed to the legend of himself as philosopher is not clear. Certainly, however, he never disowned it.

Chapter Seven

LAST PARLEYINGS OF A SOLITARY MAN

HAD Browning died at seventy-one, it would have been concluded no doubt that in the last years of his life his inspiration had waned, that his subtlety and mature insight had left him, and that mere technical ingenuity had survived. His last three volumes, however, *Ferishtah's Fancies* of 1884, *Parleyings with Certain People of Importance in Their Day* of 1887 and *Asolando*, which was published on the day of his death in 1889, testify alike to a recovery of his powers and a new deepening of his experience towards the last. For, confronted with the shadow of death, he began to take stock of his knowledge and belief, at first with some intellectual deliberation, but latterly in a more emotional way, by calling up the scenes and feelings of his youth. But *Ferishtah's Fancies* might seem to have been undertaken as a conscious counterpart to Goethe's *Westöstlicher Diwan*. The oriental convention is the same, and here, for the first time Browning elected to speak as through a mask, to distil an objective truth for a public which had begun to look to him, as had the sage of Weimar's public in his old age, for a philosophical statement. Not only is the attitude Goethe's but the somewhat elliptical lyrics set between the more discursive parables also bear traces of the German master's influence, though less direct traces than did Browning's deliberate borrowings from the second *Faust* in his 'Pisgah Sights'. For his Persian stories he reverted to his familiar blank verse, a medium whose beat seemed to have weakened a little with time. Yet there are moments when his rather colourless, imageless narration suddenly pulses at the old pace. 'Why, hate!' he demands in his 'Pillar at Sebzevar,' a poem that rates love above the pursuit of knowledge,

> If out of sand comes sand and nought but sand
> Affect not to be quaffing at mirage,
> Nor nickname pain as pleasure. That, belike,
> Constitutes just the trial of thy wit
> And worthiness to gain promotion,—hence,
> Proves the true purpose of thine actual life.
> Thy soul's environment of things perceived,
> Things visible and things invisible,
> Fact, fancy—all was purposed to evolve
> This and this only—was thy wit of worth
> To recognize the drop's use, love the same
> And loyally declare against mirage
> Though all the world asseverated dust
> Was good to drink?

The message that Browning proclaims in *Ferishtah's Fancies* is something more than a declaration against belief in mirages. Deliberately he seems to be limiting his claims, husbanding that minimum of his spiritual resources in which he could ultimately count. There is no affirmation as far-reaching as that of 'Easter Day,' none as positive in its exposition as 'A Death in the Desert.' The best single poem in the book 'A Bean Stripe; also, Apple-eating,' limits itself to recommending a withholding of judgment, to a stressing of man's ignorance. No experience is purely black or white. Our very scheme of goodness is a fiction. But it is a fiction created by God within the human mind, and of God all we can know for certain is that He is working there for truth with a force as impersonal as gravity, a force which proclaims itself in the works of great men and in the glory of the stars. The sense within us that we owe a debt does not vouch for the existence of someone ready to take his due. 'See,' he begins in a phrase that was later to find an echo in one of G. M. Hopkins' sonnets,

>   See! stars are out—
> Stars which, unconscious of thy gaze beneath,
> Go glorying, and glorify thee too
> —Those Seven Thrones, Zurah's beauty, weird Parwin!
> Whether shall love and praise to stars be paid
> Or—say—some Mubid who, for good to thee
> Blind at thy birth, by magic all his own
> Opened thine eyes, and gave the sightless sight,
> Let the stars' glory enter?

Praise is due not to the glory of the firmament but to the unseen image who gave man the gift of sight. The poem ends with a homely comparison:

>   Him
> I thank—but for whose work, the orchard's wealth
> Might prove so many gall-nuts—stocks or stones
> For aught that I should think, or know, or care.

The subject of the interspersed lyrics is human love; each of them is connected thematically with the parable it follows, and each recalls the poet's own experience in the past. For here he abandons his tales of imaginary lovers and speaks of what he has known, reverting in the lyric that follows 'A Pillar at Sebzevar' to the motive of silent adoration, pleading in another for leave to love with his whole being, body as well as soul, and speaking in a third of love as the sure guide through the recesses of another's heart:

> You groped your way across my room i' the dear dark dead of night;
> At each fresh step a stumble was: but, once your lamp alight,
> Easy and plain you walked again: so soon all wrong grew right!

The themes of love recollected and faith reduced to its very skeleton alternate rather than interlock in the course of the book. But in the 'Epilogue' they are brought together in the form of a question he had never framed before, a question whose relationship to the more discursive searchings of *Christmas Eve and Easter Day* is demonstrated by the appearance of a familiar simile. For the intimations he receives of some divine purpose working in man recall to him that image of the moon emerging from clouds that had marked his moments of vision in those early poems.

> Only, when I do hear, sudden circle round me
>   —Much as when the moon's might frees a space from cloud—
> Iridescent splendours: gloom—would else confound me—
>   Barriered off and banished far—bright-edged the blackest shroud! . . .
>
> Then the cloud-rift broadens, spanning earth that's under,
>   Wide our world displays its worth, man's strife and strife's success:
> All the good and beauty, wonder crowning wonder,
>   Till my heart and soul applaud perfection, nothing less.

But now, in his old age, he wonders whether even this apparent certainty is not a subjective experience, born of his own love rather than vouched for by any external reality.

Last Parleyings of a Solitary Man

> Only, at heart's utmost joy and triumph, terror
> Sudden turns the blood to ice: a chill wind disencharms
> All the late enchantment! What if all be error—
> If the halo irised round my head were, Love, thine arms?

But, it seems, the doubt is immediately assuaged. Even if the love he had known were the poet's only evidence of the divine purpose it would be enough. Such is the sense of his 'Epilogue's' concluding verse. Yet there is something unsatisfactory about its last line. The tension rises through the first three lines, the two dull 'ud' sounds of 'sudden' and 'blood', followed by the falling away of short 'i' sounds in 'chill,' 'wind' and 'disencharms,' and the repetition of sound from a rising to a falling rhythm in 'disencharms' and 'enchantment,' prepare for the shrill and despairing 'What if all be error?' which finds no answer in the muffled and plethoric last line. This 'Epilogue' is, I think, the record of a most profound questioning that did not find an immediate answer.

Parleyings with certain People of Importance in their Day was dedicated to the memory of yet another of Browning's lifelong friends, his French critic Milsand, who had died in the year before its publication. In the year before that, Alfred Domett, Browning's oldest friend of all, had passed away. In October 1877 Pen, whose painting had not won him patrons, and who now at the age of thirty-eight was still dependent upon his father, married a wealthy American heiress. Browning's letter to his son congratulating him on his engagement testifies to his continued preoccupation with the feckless fellow's fortunes.

'You are just at the time of life when you may "take a fresh departure" with the greatest advantage. You can bring all your acquired Continental knowledge to bear on an English enterprise: take a house and studio here, and try what may be done when your work may have the chances which you never yet enjoyed—of being seen, as you produce them, in your own studio, with the advantage of acquaintance with all the artists you care to know. Miss C. (Fanny Codrington, his fiancée) has spoken to me with the greatest frankness and generosity of the means she will have of contributing to your support—for my part, I can engage to give you £300 a year . . .'

But despite the poet's businesslike provision his son did not make his name as a painter. Miss Codrington's fortune and the royalties from his father's books were to prove sufficient to keep him in elegant and amateurish idleness. Perhaps too much had been asked of him as a child; he seems to have had no talents except a capacity for being unabashed by his own failure.

A month or two before the wedding Browning moved from his house overlooking the Regent's Canal to a larger one in De Vere Gardens. His books sold steadily and, with Pen settled, his obligations were small. A year or two before, he had endeavoured to buy a decrepit Venetian palace, in order that Pen should have 'sunshine and beauty about him, and every help to profit by them.' The old poet was growing exceedingly fond of Venice. There and in St. Moritz and in the Savoy Alps he and his sister spent their summers and autumns. Not till the last did his health seem to be failing; a hale old man, though subject to increasingly heavy colds, he replaced his old friends with new acquaintances; his visitors book read like a page from the *Almanach de Gotha*. Yet among the noble names were still those of the great writers of his time, and of the little personal following of almost professional Browning lovers.

Last Parleyings of a Solitary Man

It was his loneliness in the midst of so much distinguished company that the poet turned back to speak with some of his very earliest friends, the men whom he had first met in the books of his father's library. He had a phenomenal memory. Edmund Gosse indeed instances the picturesque account he gave towards the end of his life of a headache he had suffered from at the age of twenty-one. Gosse uses the anecdote as testimony to Browning's phenomenal freedom from illness. But set beside his *Parleyings* and his autobiographical 'Development' in his last volume of all, it tells of an increasing preoccupation in old age with the task of calling up the past. The *Parleyings* are, as was remarked in the second chapter of this study, his *Dichtung und Wahrheit*, a stock-taking as careful as that which had reduced his burden of belief to the minimum in *Ferishtah's Fancies* and its 'Epilogue.' But along with a close examination of the past went an amazing clarity. The people with whom the poet parleys are shadows; only their arguments remain. But in discussion with these, his dead masters of the past, Browning stumbled upon new discoveries, and on one especially that was to be rediscovered independently and much exploited by the psychological theorists of our own century. For in his parleying with the Walloon art historian Gerard de Lairesse, Browning elaborated the thought that mythology, which had once presented the old outward panorama of gods and immortals, had now become inward and psychological:

> If we no longer see as you of old,
> 'Tis we see deeper . . .

he informed his long dead master, in terms that seem to prophesy the subjective interpretations of the old tales that are a principal theme in Rilke's poetry, and that have lately been vulgarized on the French commercial stage. Lairesse, in his day, could not refrain from using them as a mere embellishment, an error which Browning condoned even as he pointed it out. 'Make it plain to me,' he demanded, 'why you

> poured rich life
> On what were else a dead ground—nothingness—
> Until the solitary world grew rife
> With Joves and Junos, nymphs and satyrs. Yes,
> The reason was, fancy composed the strife
> 'Twixt sense and soul: for sense, my De Lairesse,
> Cannot content itself with outward things,
> Mere beauty: soul must needs know whence there springs—
> How, when and why—what sense but loves, nor lists
> To know at all.

De Lairesse's practice was right in his century. But now the poet's visions are capable of no such pallid embodiments. They are no longer concerned with calling up the past, but with hope for the future.

The *Parleyings* contain other thoughts that extend past the discoveries of Browning's maturity. But the territory into which he was now moving was one that he was never completely to master. There are of course also repetitions, perhaps rather more concise and objective, of early motives: a return, for example, to the theme of *Fifine* in the 'Parleyings with Daniel Bartoli.' Here the widowed de Lassay, failing to remember the wife he had lost,

> took again, for better or for worse,
> The old way in the world, and, much the same
> Man o' the outside, fairly played life's game . . .

while the duke, who had renounced this same woman that had become de Lassay's wife, is haunted by a spectre

of another sort, a more resplendent and less wayward
Fifine, whose connection with Lady Ashburton is less
carefully concealed than was that of his gipsy temptress,
half woman, half girl. The quotation opens with that
familiar image which is always a sign of a heightened
subjectivity in Browning's thought:

> The duke reviewed his memories, and aghast
> Found that the Present intercepts the Past
> With such effect as when a cloud enwraps
> The moon and, moon-suffused, plays moon perhaps
> To who walks under, till comes, late or soon,
> A stumble: up he looks, and lo, the moon
> Calm, clear, convincingly herself once more!
> How could he 'scape the cloud that thrust between
> Him and effulgence? Speak, fool—duke, I mean!

And the duke speaks:

> Who bade you come, brisk-marching bold she-shape,
>   A terror with those black-balled worlds of eyes,
> That black hair bristling solid-built from nape
>   To crown it coils about? O dread surmise!
> Take, tread on, trample under past escape
>   Your capture, spoil and trophy! Do—devise
> Insults for one who, fallen once, ne'er shall rise!

Suddenly the emotional tension of the poem is as strong
as that of 'Childe Roland'. For while intending to call up
the harmless ghost of Daniel Bartoli from the day of his
childhood, Browning had summoned instead the very
incarnation of the world's sway, a figure who could
obscure the moon of his own memories, and bring with
her something of the chill terror that he had not been
able to dismiss by the halting reassurance of the last line
of his *Ferishtah* 'Epilogue'—whose weakness, significantly
enough, is repeated in the defective last line of the

quotation. Perhaps occasionally now Browning's ear was beginning to fail him. But there is a surprising strength of feeling that arises again and again in the *Parleyings*; in the attack on Disraeli in 'George Bubb Dodington,' and in the magnificent and moving landscapes in 'Gerard de Lairesse,' the eighth and ninth sections of which, with their picture of the storm and the clear morning that follows, have an effect comparable to Beethoven's in his *Pastoral Symphony*. There is indeed a quality about this description that Browning had hardly bettered since the time of *Sordello*:

> But morning's laugh sets all the crags alight
> Above the baffled tempest: tree and tree
> Stir themselves from the stupor of the night,
> And every strangled branch resumes its right
> To breathe, shakes loose dark's clinging dregs, waves free
> In dripping glory. Prone the runnels plunge,
> While earth, distent with moisture like a sponge,
> Smokes up, and leaves each plant its gem to see,
> Each grass-blade's glory-glitter. Had I known
> The torrent now turned river?—masterful
> Making its rush o'er tumbled ravage—stone
> And stub which barred the froths and foams: no bull
> Ever broke bounds in formidable sport
> More overwhelmingly, till lo, the spasm
> Sets him to dare that last mad leap: report
> Who may—his fortunes in the deathly chasm
> That swallows him in silence!

The *Parleyings* contain many passages of this packed alliterative texture. It is as if Browning has at last solved the technical problems that had obscured so many of his lines till now. The verse is compact, yet the meaning is clear. But the poems as a whole do not live up to

Last Parleyings of a Solitary Man

their surprising best. Nowhere, perhaps, is the argument so tiresomely involved as that of *Prince Hohenstiel-Schwangau*, yet there is a great deal more discursive reasoning than the emotional passages can atone for. None of the poems is an organic whole. For the personages do not come to life, and it is only a framework of human character that can hold a dramatic monologue together. But in parleying with his ghosts Browning evoked old feelings in strange new strength. No longer did he require reassurances; the object of his demands was no 'fresh knowledge' nor

> Fuller truth yet, new gainings from the grave.
> Here we alive must needs deal fairly, turn
> To what account Man may Man's portion, learn
> Man's proper play with truth in part, before
> Entrusted with the whole . . .

Now that death was near, he was confident that more truth would be revealed to him beyond the grave. In his *Parleyings* he seems to be preparing his baggage for the journey, cutting himself down to the minimum of belief and knowledge in order to travel light. At the same time he no longer found it needful to turn his eyes away from any memories; the shadowy, sexless temptress Fifine yielded to the 'bold she-shape' in 'Daniel Bartoli'; and the country took on the vivid colours of a landscape seen for the last time in 'Gerard de Lairesse.' Moreover, his verbal mastery had returned to him now, though but fitfully; only the poet's sense of character had not revived.

Asolando, Browning's last volume of poems, contains little on a level with the best of the *Parleyings* except his final 'Epilogue.' The world was now empty: all that remained was a speculative hope of the renewed presence, beyond death, of Elizabeth Browning. There is humour in one or two poems and certainly some strength still in the ironic 'Imperante Augusto Natus est—,' a poem which treats once more the theme of 'Cleon,' of the classical world's ignorance of the miracle that was taking place in its midst. But at the last the poet's vein was retrospective; he looked back on the intimations he had received, not like Wordsworth in his childhood, but in his maturity:

> And now? The lambent flame is—where?
>   Lost from the naked world: earth, sky,
> Hill, vale, tree, flower,—Italia's rare
>   O'er-running beauty crowds the eye—
> But flame? The Bush is bare.

Nevertheless, in his 'Epilogue,' despite its halting rhythms, there is a sense of courage and achievement. Here perhaps he overstates his case. But he knew that he had no cause to ask for pity, that he had lived his life richly and at the end borne his solitariness with dignity and in hope. But more perfect than his 'Epilogue,' and more suitable as a final quotation, are the last verses of 'Prospice,' a poem on the same theme of death, which had appeared in his *Dramatis Personae* twenty-five years before:

> For sudden the worst turns the best to the brave,
>   The black minute's at end,
> And the elements' rage, the fiend-voices that rave,
>   Shall dwindle, shall blend,
> Shall change, shall become first a peace out of pain,
>   Then a light, then thy breast,
> O thou soul of my soul! I shall clasp thee again,
>   And with God be the rest!

When the time came for leaving England in 1889, his seventy-eighth year, the poet was more reluctant than usual to set out. His health was now failing, and he thought that Scotland might be a more suitable place than Italy for spending the summer. But his son was established in Venice and a friend had invited him to stay at Asolo, Pippa's Asolo, which gave its name to his last volume. Here he was happy among his memories, playing on an old spinet, writing to the last and reading aloud from Shakespeare, Shelley, or his own *Ring and the Book*. He no longer talked of serious matters, but gossiped with his hostess and the sculptor Story, who had been his friend for forty years. So charmed was he with the place that he entered into negotiations to purchase a site in the town on which to build himself a house. As winter drew on, however, he left for Venice to join his son and daughter-in-law, and there he caught a bronchial cold and, as he was recovering from it, died of heart failure. On that day *Asolando* was published in London, and on the last day of the year the poet's body was buried in Westminster Abbey.

Chapter Eight

THE UNACKNOWLEDGED MASTER

'I NEVER designedly tried to puzzle people, as some of my critics have supposed,' wrote the poet to W. G. Kingsland, the future author of *Robert Browning: Chief Poet of the Age*, at a time when he was writing *The Ring and the Book*. 'On the other hand I never pretended to offer such literature as should be substitute for a cigar, or a game of dominoes to an idle man. So perhaps on the whole I get my deserts and something over . . .' The early controversies about Browning's poetry centred on its obscurities. Landor, Tennyson, his old friend Arnould, were all puzzled by the congested nature of his line, the causes for which were clearly explained by Swinburne when he observed: 'He never thinks but at full speed; and the rate of his thought is to that of another man's as the speed of a railway to that of a waggon, or the speed of a telegraph to that of a railway.' It was of a piece with his volubility in company, his excitable gestures, his occasional fits of anger. Much of his writing was hasty, many lines still seem needlessly elliptical. But the obscurity of Browning's verse was a lesser problem to succeeding generations than to men of his own time, whom he answered most cogently in a letter to Ruskin dealing with that critic's strictures on *Men and Women*.

'We don't read poetry the same way, by the same law; it is too clear. I cannot begin writing poetry till

The Unacknowledged Master

my imaginary reader has conceded licenses to me which you demur at altogether. I *know* that I don't make out my conception by my language: all poetry being a putting the infinite within the finite. You would have me paint it all plain out, which can't be; but by various artifices I try to make shift with touches and bits of outlines which *succeed* if they bear the conception from me to you. You ought, I think, to keep pace with the thought tripping from ledge to ledge of my "glaciers", as you call them; not stand poking your alpenstock into the holes, and demonstrating that no foot could have stood there;— suppose it sprang over there? In *prose* you may criticize so—because that is the absolute representation of portions of truth, what chronicling is to history—but in asking for more *ultimates* you must accept less *mediates* . . .'

But many of Browning's critics were far less consequent in their objections than Ruskin, some of them indeed hugging the lowest levels of misunderstanding, and others raising Ruskin's objections in cruder form. One compared the verse of *Strafford* to the staccato speech of Mr. Jingle; another, also turning to Dickens for his analogy, considered Browning to have adopted 'the random style of address of Mrs. Nickleby.' The prize for irrelevant incomprehension, however, should go to the critic of *Fraser's Magazine* whose viewpoint was as perverse as it is now entertaining: 'There are fine ballads,' he says, 'healthy and English, clear of that Italian-esque pedantry, that *crambe repetita* of olives and lizards, artists and monks, with which the English public, for its sins, has been spoon-fed for the last half-century, ever since Childe Harold in a luckless hour thought a warmer climate might make him a better man . . .'

But *Christmas Eve and Easter Day* stimulated misconceptions which were much more lasting than a critic's mere objections to that 'indescribable savour of the Continent,' which *Fraser's* man found in the early lyrics. These two poems of 1850 founded the awkward legend of Browning's message, of certain theological lessons which could be learnt from his poetry. But the exact nature of his message was far from clear, and discussion of his beliefs very often blinded his readers to the virtues of his poetry. Was he or was he not a Christian? The evidence was conflicting. On the one side he was a very irregular church-goer, attending the French reformed service with Milsand in Normandy or the Waldensian chapel in Venice, but seldom visiting any place of worship in London; and for additional proof of his apparent unbelief there was his thunderous 'No,' to Robert Buchanan's categorical question: 'Are you a Christian?' On the other side there was a letter written to an unknown correspondent in 1876, who imagined herself to be dying, and in this there seems to be a fundamental affirmation of Christian faith. But Browning was clearly an eclectic, accepting some Christian doctrines, passionately hostile to such ideas as eternal punishment beyond the grave, which he, nevertheless, envisaged in *The Inn Album*. Again, did Browning or did he not accept the Darwinian theory? To this he gave his own positive answer; that so much as seemed proved in it he had himself stated, before Darwin, in *Paracelsus*; that in *Luria* he had postulated 'an everlasting moment of creation, if one at all—past, present and future one and the same state'— but that he did not consider what he thought to be Darwin's case as to changes in organization, brought about by desire and will in the creature, proved.

Nevertheless, whether Browning stated his beliefs or left them in doubt, they puzzled and fascinated the generation of the nineties. Fortunately, however, his puzzling message was not the only quality for which he was read. Perhaps indeed he has never been so well loved as in the decade that followed his death. For the nineties appreciated his vigour, his sense of character and that picturesqueness which his early contemporaries had dismissed as a mere 'savour of the Continent.' All that they failed to detect was the depth of experience that underlay these several surface virtues. However, among critics of that time, Arthur Symons rated Browning second to Shakespeare alone; Walter Pater, who might have been expected to dislike the roughness of the poet's texture, spoke of 'his power of putting a happy world of his own creation in place of the meaner world of common days;' and Wilde did not disagree.

But underlying this vein of true appreciation persisted the stubborn belief that Browning was a philosophical poet, and it is this belief that turned the tide against him early in the second decade of the new century. The blame for this rests largely with the pundits of the then defunct Browning Society. For though many eminent men—Walter Raleigh, Symons, W. M. Rossetti, James Thomson, and Bernard Shaw—belonged to and addressed it, there remained a small and solid core of Browningites who considered themselves the poet's only legitimate expositors; and the Society was bent on expounding the poet's message of faith, even if that entailed the reduction of his poetic statements to plain prose meanings. Chief among the official Browningites was Mrs. Sutherland Orr, the only one who had been on terms of close friendship with the poet himself, and who had been so helped by him in the compiling of the *Handbook* that he would, in later life, refer a questioner to that book rather than attempt to answer him afresh from his own memory.

But this high priestess was herself a theist and, in many of her expositions of the poems, had subtly and no doubt unconsciously contributed to a false picture of a consistently theistic Robert Browning, a figure who failed to attract the next generation of readers. But though Mrs. Orr's unwitting misrepresentations did something to damage her master's reputation, F. J. Nettleship, in many ways a more senstive interpreter, did far more mischief. 'For us today then,' he would demand, 'what is the lesson that the poet would teach?' It was he, more than anyone, who elevated Browning into a prophet. But for all his search for ready-made morals, and calendar tag applications, Nettleship was not so wrong-headed as he seemed. He may have misrepresented Browning but at least he realized that there were deeper meanings to be found in the poetry than critics had yet discovered. Unfortunately he had a disconcerting way of reading into a given poem what theoretically should have been there; it was mistaken of him, no doubt, to go to *Fifine at the Fair* in hopes of a lesson in conduct, and even more mistaken of him to deny Fifine's attraction for Browning, and to dismiss as sophistry those parts of the poem which bore firm evidence to the contrary. But at least Nettleship was in pursuit of psychological significances that existed and could be found. He refused, for instance to accept 'Childe Roland' as a mere fantasy. Furnivall had asked the poet on three separate occasions whether there was any hidden or underlying meaning in 'Childe Roland' and three times received a denial. But Nettleship did not accept Browning's answer, and wrote a paper for the Society in which he not very successfully explored the poem for concealed significances. What is more, anticipating the psychological critics of the next century, he justified himself by quoting George Eliot to the effect that 'the words of genius bear a wider meaning than the thought which prompted them.' Browning read his article and remarked with a laugh that he supposed the meaning Nettleship found was there in the poem, though he had not known it when he wrote it. The joke seemed to be against the Browning Society pundit, whose interpretations were necessarily wild, being based rather on intellectual than psychological reasoning. But at least Nettleship's persistent search for underlying meanings was more fruitful than the succeeding generation's assumption that the poems were objective creations, and that Browning's characters, though sometimes voicing his own opinions, could not be made to give evidence concerning his true personality, attitudes or interests. Browning had himself made an inconclusive statement on this point long ago in his letter to Ruskin from which quotation has already been made. 'You may be right,' he said, 'however unwitting I am of the fact. I *may* put Robert Browning into Pippa and other men and maids. If so *peccavi*; but I don't see myself in them at all events.' Nor have his twentieth-century readers; and this blindness is one of the root causes of his contemporary neglect. For during the last forty years, at least, there has been an increasing tendency to measure the value of poetry by the intensity of the involuntary psychological confessions that can be read into it. But the statements which could be extracted from Browning's poetry were not those for which critics influenced by psycho-analysis were looking. They tended therefore to view the poet as one who consistently avoided topics that might give him away. Gerard Manley Hopkins gave weight to this accusation in a letter to Dixon, published for the first time in the thirties, in which he spoke of Browning's 'frigidities.' But Hopkins' objections were based, for the most part, on a very special set of prejudices. He criticized particular images, as Eliot later criticized Shelley's, and found them blurred. How many natural descriptions, however, he might have noticed that are as firm in outline as his own! But what chiefly exasperated him was 'Browning's way of talking (and making his people talk) with the air and spirit of a man bouncing up from table with his mouth full of bread and cheese and saying that he meant no nonsense.' This Chestertonian vice he found, quite inexplicably, at its most intense in 'The Flight of the Duchess.' But this is a mere surface objection, not founded on a consideration of Browning's work as a whole; it could not possibly be made to apply to *The Ring and the Book*. It is, I think, no more than a mere casual cover for a much more fundamental distaste for Browning's protestantism, for his steadfast attempts to see reality not through the eyes of a Church or a tradition, but through those of a man alone, self-reliant yet conscious of a single man's limitations. Browning, moreover, mixes intellect and emotion in a very different way from Hopkins or his master Donne—whom, incidentally, he greatly admired long before his poems were generally read. To Browning the essential experience was emotional, and only its exposition intellectual; Donne and Hopkins, on the other hand, to quote T. S. Eliot's words, felt their thought as immediately as the odour of a rose. This distinction between the intellectual and the reflective poet is, however, a psychological one only, with no importance in the field of values. Hopkins' intolerance of his elder contemporary was based on no serious attempt at value judgment. It was the prejudice of a man of different faith and different attitudes, and a prejudice that he could not always sustain. 'The Brownings are very fine too,' he admitted once, 'in their ghastly way.' It was a reluctant and half-hearted confession, but no more than was due to the author of *Pacchiarotto*, who in light-hearted mood had prepared the way for Hopkins' own masterly word combinations—for such neologisms as trambeam, rook-racked, arch-especial. Little as Hopkins liked Browning's beliefs—which he condemned as Broad Church —or his reflective attitudes, he had considerable respect for his technique.

But the 'intellectual' line of attack did not develop until Browning's reputation had already slumped. Hopkins' letters were not published till the nineteen-thirties. The real enemy to his reputation was the totally false legend that his characters had very little to do with the poet himself; that they were so many voices invented for the purpose of stating some particular point of view. This 'parnassian Browning, a multiple impersonator, a master of realistic detail and didacticism' seems to Sir Maurice Bowra a sort of sententious gravedigger at the funeral of the last Romantics; better Rossetti with his laudanum and his flowing cloak than that well-dressed dapper old gentleman with a sound taste in Rhine wines. For Professor Tillyard, a representative critic, perhaps, of the other University, Browning is capable of expressing the small social and moral commonplaces, the more quotidian of the human passions, but lacks that obliquity of approach, that knack of saying several things at once, without which, according to the Cambridge school, nothing profound can be expressed.

But alongside accusations of parnassian dullness and petty realism, there run even graver charges of psychological falsity. F. L. Lucas, the chief prosecutor in this court, clearly enjoys certain of Browning's lyrics, but he is repelled by what he considers the poet's optimistic misconceptions concerning the world. For Mr. Lucas likes his poetry to be melancholy and stoical, and more than suspects those of the Victorian poets who could see any hope beyond the grave. Browning, for him, is an insensitive and pompous man who after one burst of romance, out of which he made his best poetry, 'settled again into that even tenour' in which he persisted to the end. Mr. Lucas compares him indeed to his own Bishop who ordered his tomb in St. Praxed's church, alleging that they had a great deal in common, both of them being mighty appreciative of the things of this world. If only Browning had been content, this most entertaining critic implies, to rejoice like that half-pagan creature of his imagination, to enjoy things as he found them, to write love lyrics and describe the picturesque aspects of the Italian Renaissance without pointing a moral, how much better a poet he would have been. But since, for Browning, love was not merely a series of bitter-sweet transports but an experience carrying with it intimations of something even higher, and since Renaissance Italy was at best a background against which he set dramas of the human mind transcending any historical period; since the poet was more concerned with Pompilia and Caponsacchi and the Pope than with one half-Rome or the other, Mr. Lucas was in effect asking Browning to limit his talents and his insights to his secondary material, a field of which he had been complete master before he had any emotional experience at all, before he so much as met Elizabeth. For the book that this unorthodox Cambridge critic singles out for his highest praise is the *Dramatic Romances* of 1845. Mr. Lucas' attitude to the mature Robert Browning is that of the poet's own dispassionately acid *tertium quid*, reporting to his

The Unacknowledged Master

Excellency the exaggerated and vulgar behaviour of certain people who are in fact living with an intensity of which he is completely unaware. 'Browning,' says Lucas in criticizing the last 'Epilogue', 'calls the theatre of the world to take note how a Browning can live and die.' But of all Victorian poets Browning was most sparing of the first person singular; he put it behind him after *Pauline* and very seldom used it again. When he did it was because the experience he had to describe was one that he knew to be shared by his fellows.

A younger generation view Browning with yet another variety of distaste. John Heath Stubbs in his *Darkling Plain*, a book which follows the fortunes of Romanticism after the death of Byron, Shelley and Keats, gives his reasons for attempting to omit all notice of either Browning or Tennyson. In fact they bob up repeatedly in his book, like unwanted guests at a garden party. Browning, according to him, rendered poetry palatable to the earnest Puritan intellectuals of his day. But his only surviving merit for this most destructive critic is that despite his preoccupation with half-digested thought he possessed a fancy less restricted and more vigorous than Tennyson's, and therein bore a distant affinity to Beddoes. Heath Stubbs singles out 'Childe Roland' as 'a pure exercise in the horrible,' a category of thought which he considers less poetic than 'the terrible,' since it dwells not on moral evil but on sheer physical pain. The imagery of such a poem, in Heath Stubbs' opinion, contradicts the intellectual creed of courage and optimism which was the outward face that Browning turned to the world. He is, in fact, repeating in his own way Lucas' accusation of falsity. For he approaches poetry from a psycho-analytical point of view that presupposes inspiration to arise from the same 'unconscious' level as dreams: a misconception which confuses the two very distant human activities, the one purely mechanical, the other the product of some profounder intimations from a source outside man's common thoughts and feelings, the record of some emotional flash of comprehension that lights for him a universe outside that of his own fears and guilt. Heath Stubbs says that in 'An Epistle of Karshish', 'A Death in the Desert,' 'Caliban upon Setebos' neither intuitive faith nor honest doubt speaks clearly. But that is to judge Browning from a preconceived point of view, to which only the statements of Clough and Christina Rossetti seem valid. In fact there is at man's ordinary level of insight no constant mood of either faith or doubt. There are certain experiences that may serve to strengthen the one, certain aridities that make for the other. It is of these varying levels of certainty and illusion that Browning speaks through his various characters. Pompilia's sleepwalking certainty of right and wrong, the Pope's sudden emotional understanding at the end of a life of intellectual comprehension, and Caponsacchi's despairing cry, are three lightning flashes in a world where one half-Rome slanders and the other half indistinctly senses that something strange is taking place. But the vast panorama of *The Ring and the Book* required a degree of intellectual organization beyond the capacities of any of the later Romantic poets whom Heath Stubbs praises. Far from Browning's merits being, in Heath Stubbs' words, not strictly poetic, they are poetic on a far greater scale than those of Beddoes, Patmore, Christina Rossetti or Hopkins, all of whom certainly spoke with intensity but out of a more circumscribed field of experience.

Somewhat deeper in her incomprehension because

more muddled in her thinking is the advocate of 'subjective universality,' Miss Kathleen Raine, whose ideal visionary poet must 'participate in the unconscious and half-conscious imaginings of the community.' Certainly as a deep level mass-observer Browning is no more successful than as the poet of 'the terrible' which Heath Stubbs would wish him to be. For Miss Raine he is, however, 'a major poet, but a poet only in the lowest sense in which it is possible to use the word at all.' But it is difficult to attach any precise significance to a statement that really says no more than that she does not like Browning, yet is not prepared to say that he is negligible. It serves however as additional proof that contemporary critics are prone to approach Browning with preconceptions concerning the nature of poetry that make it impossible for them to accept him for what he is.

But there is a further obstacle to the appreciation of Browning that looms even larger at the present day than the objection of the psychological critics, and that is the backwash of imagist theory that still informs much poetic criticism. We have come to look too closely at the strength, originality and evocative power of the single poetic image, and to read our poetry, if not phrase by phrase, at least line by line, blind to the importance of large scale poetic organization. Browning, however, like Shakespeare and Milton, built his poems massively. Often, as Sir Maurice Bowra has pointed out, he is careless of individual words; sometimes his ear is defective and his rhythm careless, and like all Victorian poets he finds it hard to solve the problem of poetic diction. His rhythms are spoken rhythms, conceived on a basis of dramatic speech Elizabethan in its influences. His overcompression—Elizabethan too in its way—tends, as Swinburne pointed out, to make his meanings at times obscure. Never, as a lyricist, is he as certain in his language as a far lesser poet than he, William Barnes. For Barnes in his restricted way solved the problem of poetic vocabulary by returning to an uncontaminated dialect. Put 'Love among the Ruins' beside Barnes 'Fall Time', and you see the advantage of an unworked idiom over one already overrich in associations. Barnes is describing his own Dorset country:

> The rick's a tipp'd an' weather-brown'd,
>   An thatch'd wi' zedge a-dried an' dead;
> An' orcha'd apples, red half round,
>   Have all a-happer'd down, a-shed
> Underneath the tree's wide head.
>   Ladders long,
> Rong by rong, to clim' the tall
> Trees, be hung upon the wall.

The verse, at first sight simple, is elaborately organized with internal rhymes, assonances and half-rhymes. But at least one half of its freshness it owes to the unfamiliarity of its language; 'a-dried an dead,' 'a-shed,' 'be hung' in what Barnes called National English, would seem 'poetical' and trite; and it is just these old forms and inversions that mar Browning's equally well organized and subtly rhymed poem:

> And such plenty and perfection, see, of grass,
>   Never was!
> Such a carpet as, this summer-time, o'erspreads
>   And embeds
> Every vestige of the city, guessed alone,
>   Stock or stone—

Here 'o'erspreads,' legitimate in Dorset dialect, is false in National English, and 'stock or stone' raises an imprecise and literary image that lowers the tension of the verse. Purely as a lyrical poet of mood, Browning is, as Bowra says, careless in his language. For his idiom is not sufficiently pure for such small-scale purposes.

But Browning's nearest to lyrical perfection, such a poem as 'Love in a Life', contains hardly any of those archaisms and inversions that trouble our contemporary ear.

> Yet the day wears,
> And door succeeds door;
> I try the fresh fortune—
> Range the wide house from the wing to the centre.
> Still the same chance! she goes out as I enter.
> Spend my whole day in the quest,—who cares?
> But 'tis twilight you see,—with such suites to explore,
> Such closets to search, such alcoves to importune!

Yet even here is a slight roughness, no more rasping perhaps than the unexpected jolts that Hardy introduced into his lyrics to remind the reader of fate's asperities, but sufficient to prevent the poem's singing itself, as an Elizabethan lyric does. For unfortunately Browning is never so certain of himself in a light metrical form as in those more loosely constructed poems for which he adapted the double-jointed medium of Hood and Barham. In them his language is more colloquial, his poeticisms appearing, as it might be, between inverted commas. As an example of this mood, which prevails in poems as various in their emotional charge as 'The Pied Piper' and 'The Flight of the Duchess', it is worth quoting a verse from one of the far less well-known 'Garden Fancies.' in which the unfortunate volume of the pedant 'Sibrandus Schafnaburgensis' has just been fished up from a well:

> Here you have it, dry in the sun,
>   With all the binding all of a blister,
> And great blue spots where the ink has run,
>   And reddish streaks that wink and glister

O'er the page so beautifully yellow:
  Oh, well have the droppings played their tricks!
Did he guess how toadstools grow, this fellow?
  Here's one stuck in his chapter six!

How did he like it when the live creatures
  Tickled and toused and browsed him all over,
And worm, slug, eft, with serious features,
  Came in, each one for his right of trover?
—When the water beetle with great blind deaf face
  Made of her eggs the stately deposit,
And the newt borrowed just so much of the preface
  As tiled in the top of his black wife's closet?

Here Browning is using a uniform vocabulary in which he can express both his observations and his amused and intellectual comments. It is a verse form which is not capable of filling every purpose, and one reason, perhaps, for the failure of *Fifine at the Fair* was the use in it of such a diction, suitable enough for light-hearted narrative but incapable of carrying any emotional weight:

So with this wash o' the world, wherein life-long we drift;
We push and paddle through the foam by making shift
To breathe above at whiles when, after deepest duck
Down underneath the show, we put forth hand and pluck
At what seems somehow like reality—a soul.

The lines convey nothing of the metaphysical discovery they were intended to communicate. Perhaps Browning's reluctance, in that poem, to specify the exact nature of the worldly pulls that tempted him to forget his Elvire, dictated also the would-be almost casual form of the poem. But that side of Browning's talent, so long as it was applied to the writing of poems within its scope, was more certain in its mastery than was the lyrical side, in descent from Shelley, which too often just fell short of complete mastery.

By far the richest side of Browning's multiform achievement, however, was the verse of his dramatic monologues, of *The Ring and the Book*, *The Inn Album* and the *Parleyings*. This medium is, I repeat, at its loosest and flattest in 'Bishop Blougram' and *Prince Hohenstiel-Schwangau*. For Blougram's lukewarm confession of faith it has a correspondingly plain unemphatic line:

> Well now, there's one great form of Christian faith
> I happened to be born in—which to teach
> Was given me as I grew up, on all hands,
> As best and readiest means of living by;
> The same on examination being proved
> The most pronounced moreover, fixed, precise
> And absolute form of faith in the whole world—
> Accordingly, most potent of all forms
> For working on the world.

The assonances are few and unmarked; the third, fifth and sixth lines slide almost unnoticed from the blank-verse rhythm, and the whole forms an intellectual statement almost devoid of imagery. It is already three-quarters of the way to the completely unobtrusive verse of T. S. Eliot's *Cocktail Party*, to such a passage as that in which Reilly discusses the inevitability of Celia Coplestone's death:

>   The only question
> Then was, what sort of death? I could not know
> Because it was for her to choose the way of life
> To lead to death, and, without knowing the end
> Yet choose the form of death.

Eliot's rhythms depart further from those of the five-beat line, and Eliot again would not allow himself the inversion of Blougram's 'which to teach,' or the ellipsis of his fourth line. But the spoken rhythms of Eliot's play, as indeed much else in modern poetry, owe something to Browning. Ezra Pound indeed, started much under the influence of the 'old mesmerizer' who—thanks to Hood perhaps—had at times half freed himself from the tyranny of poetic diction.

> Cat's i' the water-butt! Thought's in your verse barrel,
> Tell us this thing rather, then we'll believe you,
> You, Master Bob Browning, spite your apparel
> Jump to your sense and give praise as we'd lief do.

Pound's verses are almost a parody, closer in spirit to J. K. Stephens' mocking 'Birthdays' than to genuine Browning. For Pound's attitude to his master was clearly ambivalent. But by way of Pound's influence on Eliot, and Eliot's on Auden, the blood of Browning's verse is still running in contemporary poetry, contributing an hereditary feature here and there, a grotesque twist to Robert Graves, perhaps, and an ingenious rhyme to Edith Sitwell's *Façade*. Recessive rather than dominant, he remains nevertheless an ancestor. But when we compare the quotations from 'Bishop Blougram' to that from *The Cocktail Party* we find one radical dissimilarity. Although innovating, Browning was content, even at his most conversational, to retain in his monologues the mannerisms of the Elizabethan dramatic line; for despite his contemporaneity and colloquialism Blougram is made to speak verse less free than that of 'The Flight of the Duchess'. Nevertheless, Browning's most successful medium is his blank verse line, which Blougram's monologue displays at its flattest level. It is, however, capable of developing a richness of texture to correspond

The Unacknowledged Master

to the richer thought and greater emotional conviction inspiring other poems. There is a very great contrast, indeed, between the unemphatic, imageless argument of Blougram or the Saviour of Society and the Pope's language as he gives his interpretation of Guido's plot against Pompilia:

> 'Tis done:
> Wherefore should mind misgive, heart hesitate?
> He calls to counsel, fashions certain four
> Colourless natures counted clean till now,
> —Rustic simplicity, uncorrupted youth,
> Ignorant virtue! Here's the gold o' the prime
> When Saturn ruled, shall shock our leaden day—
> The clown abash the courtier! Mark it, bards!
> The courtier tries his hand on clownship here,
> Speaks a word, names a crime, appoints a price—
> Just breathes on what, suffused with all himself,
> Is red-hot henceforth past distinction now
> I' the common glow o' hell. And thus they break
> And blaze on us at Rome, Christ's birthnight-eve!

The alliterative division of the first and second complete lines quoted: the three contemptuous dull U sounds of the fourth; and the repeated hard C's of the third and fourth picked up again in the seventh and eighth, and leading to the 'crime' of the ninth and the 'Christ' of the last; the three B's in the last two lines: all these devices show the contrived complexity of the passage, which has been constructed as a single block held together by far more than the logic of its argument and the comparative regularity of its beat.

But this brilliance of texture Browning preserved long after the writing of *The Ring and the Book*. It is every bit as rich, indeed, in such a passage as that from *The Inn Album* in which the woman reproaches her returned lover for the ruin he has brought her:

> That moment when you first revealed yourself
> My simple impulse prompted—end forthwith
> The ruin of a life uprooted thus
> To surely perish! How should such spoiled tree
> Henceforward baulk the wind of its worst sport,
> Fail to go falling deeper, falling down
> From sin to sin until some depth were reached
> Doomed to the weakest by the wickedest
> Of weak and wicked human kind?

The dead M's and P's of the first two lines, with the repeated 'IMP' of the second; the three W's of the fifth line, the F's and D's of the sixth, and seventh and eighth, and the repeated U's of the last two reinforce the heavy rhythm of inevitability that informs the whole passage.

Such was his technical mastery, and combined with it there was his sharp, penetrating vision of the external world, a vision that could catch in *Pauline*, in *Sordello* in the monologues and right into his old age, a mood of nature, a cloudscape, or the houses and streets and people of a town. His scenic detail had all its sharpness of outline still when he came at seventy-three or four to his parley with Gerard de Lairesse, an old man still celebrating the midday of his inspiration:

> Noon is the conqueror—not a spray, nor leaf,
> Nor herb, nor blossom but has rendered up
> Its morning dew: the valley seemed one cup
> Of cloud-smoke, but the vapour's reign was brief,
> Sun-smitten, see, it hangs—the filmy haze—
> Grey-garmenting the herbless mountain-side,
> To soothe the day's sharp glare: while far and wide
> Above unclouded burns the sky, one blaze
> With fierce immitigable blue, no bird
> Ventures to spot by passage . . .

Such is Browning's control of verbal sound and

recorded vision. He was, to use his own definition, an objective poet where Shelley was a subjective one. As such his appeal was to the aggregate human mind and his concern with the doings of men. So, though unsuccessful as a playwright, he was, primarily and always the poet of the dramatic situation, and a 'fashioner' before he was a 'seer.' Shelley took only from nature what struck out most abundantly and uninterruptedly his inner light and power. Browning took much more, but not, in parnassian fashion, merely for the sake of the men and scenes and cities he described. He viewed nature and humanity with ceaseless curiosity and sympathy, trying over in his poetry ever fresh combinations of character and landscape, but always with the view of discovering some secret that lay behind them. Had he pursued the course on which he embarked in *Pauline* he would have continued to lay bare his own heart in the hope of discovering the secret there; had he pursued the false trail struck in 'Christmas Eve' he would have ceaselessly argued about the ultimate nature of experience and lost his clue in a welter of mere ratiocination. As it was he embodied ever and again in fresh poetry his flashes of comprehension concerning the relations of the trinity, Love, Knowledge and Faith, which came thickest in his early maturity, but which did not desert him in his long years of outwardly barren living, and which returned with renewed strength in the years immediately before his death. Browning had indeed a philosophical message, though not one of the kind the Browning Society was looking for. The secret, he tells us again and again, is to be found in man's experience, not in abstraction but in the welter and richness, in the violence and colour, in the love and beauty of the world itself.

SHORT BIBLIOGRAPHY

This list is intended merely to denote the sources I have used most freely in the writing of this book. It will be useful to anyone wanting to read more about the poet, but it is in no sense a guide to the huge field of Browning studies, nor even a complete list of the works that I have consulted.

THE POETICAL WORKS OF ROBERT BROWNING, 2 vols. in one. John Murray.

ROBERT BROWNING: POETRY AND PROSE, edited by Simon Nowell-Smith. Rupert Hart-Davis. Reynard Library.
This contains an interesting selection from Browning's shorter poetry well-printed, the essay on Shelley and a handful of letters, including one to Ruskin reprinted from Frederick Collingwood's *Life*.

LETTERS OF ROBERT BROWNING, edited by Thurman L. Hood. John Murray.

NEW LETTERS OF ROBERT BROWNING, edited by de Vane and Knickerbocker. John Murray.

LETTERS OF ROBERT BROWNING AND ELIZABETH BARRETT, 1845–6, 2 vols. in one. John Murray.

DEAREST ISA, Robert Browning's Letters to Isabella Blagden, edited by Edward Mc Aleer. Thomas Nelson & Sons.

LETTERS OF ELIZABETH BARRETT BROWNING, edited by F. G. Kenyon. 2 vols. The Macmillan Co., New York.

LETTERS OF ELIZABETH BARRETT BROWNING TO HER SISTER, 1846–1859, edited by Leonard Huxley. John Murray.

ROBERT BROWNING'S PERSONALIA, by Edmund Gosse. T. Fisher Unwin.

ROBERT BROWNING, by William Sharp. Walter Scott.

LIFE AND LETTERS OF ROBERT BROWNING, by Mrs. Sutherland Orr. John Murray.

Short Bibliography

HANDBOOK TO ROBERT BROWNING'S WORKS, by Mrs. Sutherland Orr. George Bell & Sons.

LIFE OF ROBERT BROWNING, by Edward Dowden. Everyman. J. M. Dent.

BROWNING'S BACKGROUND AND CONFLICT, by F. R. G. Duckworth. Ernest Benn.

LIFE OF ROBERT BROWNING, by W. Hall Griffin, completed and edited by H. C. Minchin. Methuen.

BIOGRAPHICAL AND CRITICAL STUDIES, by James Thomson. Dobell.

ROBERT BROWNING'S EARLY FRIENDS, by S. K. Ratcliffe. The Cornhill No. 979. Summer 1949.

NOTE

The following books, which have appeared since the first publication of this one, contain interesting material on the poet:

ROBERT BROWNING: A Portrait, by Betty Miller. John Murray, 1952. This is a biography, somewhat psycho-analytical in tone, but by far the best modern account of the poet.

AMPHIBIAN: A Reconsideration of Browning, by Henry Charles Duffin. Bowes and Bowes, 1956. This contains interesting assessments of many poems, joins issue with some previous critics and devotes a special appendix to refuting Mrs Miller.

BROWNING'S CHARACTERS: A Study in Poetic Technique, by Park Honan, Yale University Press, 1961. This is a very thorough investigation of Browning's sense of character and his technique in the dramatic monologue.

INDEX

Abt Vogler, 108, 109
Agamemnon of Aeschylus, The, 123, 151
Andrea del Sarto, 90
Apparent Failure, 107
Aristophanes' Apology, 145–146
Artemis Prologizes, 31
Asolando, 161, 171–173

Balaustion's Adventure, including a Transcript from Euripides, 122–125, 133
Bifurcation, 149
Bishop Blougram's Apology, 92–94, 96, 189–190
Bishop Orders his Tomb in St. Praxed's, The, 34–35, 56, 182
Blot in the 'Scutcheon, A, 3
By the Fireside, 87

Caliban upon Setebos, 106–7, 184
Cavalier Tunes, 35
'Childe Roland to the Dark Tower came', 77–82, 176, 183
Christmas Eve and Easter Day, 49, 53, 56–57, 62–68, 70, 73, 176
Cleon, 76, 90, 91–92
Colombe's Birthday, 32, 134
Cristine, 29
Cristine and Monaldeschi, 156

Death in the Desert, A, 76, 83, 88, 110–11, 184
De Gustibus, 37
Development, 167
Dramatic Idyls (First and second series), 156–157
Dramatic Lyrics, 25
Dramatic Romances and Lyrics, 34–45, 182
Dramatis Personae, 105–112]

Epilogue to '*Asolando*', 172, 183

Epilogue to '*Dramatis Personae*', 108
Epistle, An, containing the Strange Medical Experience of Karshish the Arab Physician, 6 76–77, 83, 96, 184

Ferishtah's Fancies, 8, 149, 161, 162–165, 167, 169
Fifine at the Fair, 130, 136–140, 156, 176, 188
Flight of the Duchess, The, 39–45, 51, 53, 54–55, 180, 187
Fra Lippo Lippi, 56, 90–91

Grammarian's Funeral, A, 108
Guardian Angel, The, 75

Heretic's Tragedy, The, 74
Home Thoughts from Abroad, 37
Home Thoughts from the Sea, 1, 37
House, 12, 150
How they Brought the Good News, 2

'Imperante Augusto natus est', 172
In a Gondola, 29
Inn Album, The, 146–148, 149, 176, 191–2
Italian in England, The, 60
Ixion, 156

Johannes Agricola, 23, 54
Jocoseria, 130, 156

King Victor and King Charles, 22

La Saisiaz, 130, 148, 152–153, 155
Last Ride Together, The, 89
Life in a Love, 89
Lost Leader, The, 1
Love among the Ruins, 76, 84, 186
Love in a Life, 89, 187
Lovers' Quarrel, A, 89
Luria, 32, 50, 56, 176

Index

Master Hugues of Saxe-Gotha, 85–86
May and Death, 107
Men and Women, 73–97, 98, 99, 101, 132, 149
Mr. Sludge 'the Medium', 100, 105–106
My Last Duchess, 30, 56

Nationality in Drinks, 37
Never the Time and the Place, 156

One Word More, 89–90

Pacchiarotto and How he Worked in Distemper, etc., 149, 156, 181
Paracelsus, 15–18, 58, 59, 176
Parleyings with Certain People of Importance in Their Day, 9, 11–12, 44, 161, 165, 167–171, 192
Pauline, 4, 9, 13–14, 18
Pictor Ignotus, 35–36
Pied Piper of Hamelin, The, 2, 3, 6, 25–26, 187
Pippa Passes, 1, 4, 23–25, 56
Pisgah sights, 150, 162
Porphyria's Lover, 1, 23, 54
Prince Hohenstiel-Schwangau, Saviour of Society, 102, 125–130, 189

Prospice, 108, 172

Rabbi ben Ezra, 108–109, 110
Red Cotton Nightcap Country, 141–145, 149
Return of the Druses, The, 22
Ring and the Book, The, 2, 3, 5, 7, 112–122, 130, 149, 159, 180, 184, 191

St. Martin's Summer, 149
Saul, 38–39, 51
Shelley's Letters, Introduction to, 97
Sibrandus Schafnaburgensis, 187
Soliloquy of the Spanish Cloister, 25, 54
Song, 'The Moth's Kiss First', 30, 53
Sordello, 4, 19–21, 101
Soul's Tragedy, A, 33, 50, 56
Statue and the Bust, The, 56
Strafford, 18–19, 175

'Transcendentalism', 73
Two Poets of Croisic, The, 153–154

Waring, 25, 28
Why I am a Liberal, 128
Woman's Last Word, A, 149
Women and Roses, 74–75, 83